CHAUCER AND HIS POETRY

CHAUCER
AND HIS
POETRY

BY

GEORGE LYMAN KITTREDGE

Fifty-fifth Anniversary Edition
with an Introduction by B. J. Whiting

HARVARD UNIVERSITY PRESS

CAMBRIDGE, MASSACHUSETTS

1970

CONTENTS

INTRODUCTION

BY B. J. WHITING

THE introduction to the fifteenth printing of *Chaucer and His Poetry*[1] has two purposes, first, to suggest reasons for the continued and steady demand for the book and, second, to say something about the author. It is not a compressed biography — the life and the legend are set forth by Clyde K. Hyder[2] — or a list of writings — these are given fully in James Thorpe's bibliography.[3] Rather it is an attempt, however imperfect and disordered, to depict Kittredge as he lives nearly thirty years after his death in the memories of his devoted students, now themselves in middle age or beyond.

Chaucer and His Poetry first appeared in 1915, fifty-five years ago, and in that year its

[1] In this printing the quotations from Chaucer have been adjusted to the text as given in F. N. Robinson, ed., *The Works of Geoffrey Chaucer*, Boston, Houghton Mifflin, 1957.

[2] Clyde K. Hyder, *George Lyman Kittredge, Teacher and Scholar*, Lawrence, Kansas, 1962. Hyder includes a fine assortment of the stories, not all of them apocryphal, in which Kittredge figures.

[3] *A Bibliography of the Writings of George Lyman Kittredge*, Cambridge, Massachusetts, 1948. This volume has a charming introduction by Hyder E. Rollins, one of Kittredge's favorite students.

author, George Lyman Kittredge, was fifty-five years old. Although the numerological value of the coincidence is probably slight, it reminds us that the book has worn well and that it was the product not of either nonage or dotage but of fully developed scholarly and critical powers. Kittredge was a founder and one of the first Syndics of Harvard University Press, the publisher of the work, and the Press is now housed in a building named Kittredge Hall in his honor.

Academic lectures, even when transferred to the printed page, frequently have an ephemeral quality, and while this is fortunately not a universal rule, there are few which have been in print for more than half a century. John Quincy Adams, Harvard's first Boylston Professor of Rhetoric and Oratory, remarked upon the appearance of his lectures in book form that "To live in the memory of mankind by college lectures is not the aim of a very soaring ambition." Adams' course lectures, to be sure, were well enough prepared to be printed without revision, as were Kittredge's Turnbull Lectures, but here the similarity ends. The *Lectures on Rhetoric and Oratory* fell flat from the press and have been little read since. *Chaucer and His Poetry* has stayed in print beyond most of Kittredge's other works, and this without the artificial aid of required reading lists. To ask why is natural, and it is not difficult to propose answers. The term *haute vulgarisation* might have been invented for the book. By 1914, when the lectures were delivered, Kittredge had written extensively on Chaucer and had, indeed, published or prepared almost all of his research on the poet. Here is a distillation of years of study and thought, yet so artful, at once guileless and guileful, that the weight of scholarship is never felt. There has rarely been such a satisfying and gentle introduction to the work and times of a poet. The fabled general reader is accommodated from the start. No advance knowledge is required. The quotations are often translated or paraphrased. Honest and useful relevance is stressed. The very absence of the panoply of scholarship is helpful, since nothing ages like a learned footnote. Of paramount importance are the clarity of style, intended for the ear yet responsive to the eye, and the persuasive presentation of fact and argument.

Kittredge's views have been challenged, at some times more successfully than at others. To controvert an eminent scholar can win recognition if not acceptance. The Dreamer in the *Book of the Duchess*, allegory in the

House of Fame, the genre of the *Troilus,* the *Canterbury Tales* as an incipient drama, a Human Comedy, the extent or even the presence of the Marriage Group, the character of the Pardoner — all these and more have been explained or interpreted in other and frequently differing ways. Not so long ago a graduate student who had been examining a lustrum's accumulation of Chaucer studies observed that much current research seemed to consist of footnotes to Kittredge. All this would be pleasing rather than otherwise to Kittredge, who was more interested than outraged by competing theories. Of one assault on his Dreamer he said benignly, "Very plausible, but I stick to my guns."

Fifty-five years is a long time by any standards short of Methuselah's or Old Parr's, and 1970 is not perhaps a year in which to predict the future of traditional literary interests, and thus the standing of *Chaucer and His Poetry* fifty-five years from now can be left, safely enough, to the executrice of wyrdes. An unbiased judgment, that of one not in a position to receive royalties from the publisher or thanks from the author, is that the book will be in print in 2025. Until a better appears, *Chaucer and His Poetry* is the best first step to Chaucer for a reader unacquainted

with the poet. If he is incited to go on, as
many will be, he will learn that much has been
written about Chaucer since 1915, and he can
balance Kittredge's judgments against those
of later prophets. If, on the other hand, he is
content to be a man of one book, it will make
little difference, least of all to him, if he
accepts, say, the Dreamer in Kittredge's
terms. One thing is as sure as things can be:
those who begin *Chaucer and His Poetry*
finish it.

Scholars frequently reflect, wistfully or
smugly, that the lives of persistent scholars,
at least in the humanities, rarely contain
episodes attractive to the lively biographer.
Kittredge was no exception. His private life
was happy and uneventful; his public life,
if it may be called that, was confined to the
classroom and the lecture platform. Letters,
once the core, and sometimes the upas tree,
of the academic's biography, were not his
customary way of communication. A post-
card, rarely filled, served his need, and here he
followed F. J. Furnivall rather than F. J. Child.

Kittredge was born in Boston in 1860 of
what Clough calls "the New England ancient
blood," but the truly formative days of his
youth were spent in Barnstable on Cape Cod.

Barnstable, then a small, cohesive community of year-round residents, was the home of his mother's people and here, in addition to frequent shorter visits, he lived from his thirteenth to his fifteenth year. From Barnstable came his lifelong interest in the early history of New England, its records and its folklore, tales more than twice-told of Dark Days and moon-cursers, of doctors, ministers, and soldiers, of ghosts, witches, and wizards, and in such tangible relics as arrows of Indians and their skeletons. One massive segment of Kittredge's writings may not unreasonably be traced to Barnstable: his studies in Colonial history and, notably, *The Old Farmer and his Almanac* (1904), that most readable and eclectic preface to an older New England, and the magisterial *Witchcraft in Old and New England* (1929). Barnstable's present did as much for the boy as its past, because, unlike Boston, it was a classless society with but the frailest barriers between families and between youth and age, so that he came to know ordinary people, as ordinary and ornery as New Englanders can be. His later life, for that matter, was spent in a one-class society, but the class was as artificial as it was admirable, and Kittredge would never have had the understanding of human nature which leavened his criticism, written and above all in the classroom, had it not been for Barnstable, where he was to spend almost every summer and where he died in 1941.[4]

The family returned to Boston and Kittredge went to the Roxbury Latin School (1875-1878) and then to Harvard (1878-1882). That the first scholar in his class at Roxbury should major in the classics at Harvard and be again the first scholar in his class was natural enough. Less predictable was his popularity among his fellows and his active part in clubs, feasts, and periodicals. He was a witty after-dinner speaker, a ready writer of parody and burlesque, and a facile rhymester. Almost forgotten is the fact that in 1895 he gave the annual Phi Beta Kappa poem entitled "Philosophy the Guide," an effusion which he did not see fit to print. Almost as obscured by time is his spirit of playfulness. Like his undergraduate teacher and lifelong friend, Le Baron Russell Briggs, he understood the meaning of *dulce est desipere in loco*. As a child he projected a publication to be called *Poetry and Fun*; as a man he delighted in quoting Artemus Ward. His after-dinner remarks,

[4] An affectionate picture of Barnstable in the 1960's is by Kurt Vonnegut, Jr., *Welcome to the Monkey House* (New York, 1970), pp. 1-6.

often off-the-cuff, were marked by comic learning and inoffensively facetious personalities.

If there is such a thing as a genuine turning point in a man's life, that time came to Kittredge in the fall of 1880 when he enrolled in English 4, Francis James Child's course in Middle English. Child's *Ballads* keep his name alive, even if some of those who could not work without him damn him with faint praise, but, partly because his life was never written, the man and teacher have become shadowy. Today, despite our horde of political and evangelical professors, it is not easy to realize the love and reverence in which Child was held far beyond his accustomed course between Kirkland Street and the College Yard. From what used to be called humble origins, his father a sailmaker and his playground the Boston wharves, he came to be the first internationally recognized American scholar in the humanities and a man of whom William James could say, "He had a moral delicacy and a richness of heart that I never saw and never expect to see equalled," and "I loved Child more than any man I know." Child was a short, stocky man, called "Stubby" by half a century of students, with a full head of light, curly hair. Despite his quiet, un-

assuming manner he had an infectious enthusiasm that drew people to him and to the
things with which he was concerned. Once
when he agreed to add extra hours to his
exposition of Chaucer and said that his
students might, if they liked, invite friends,
the auditors swelled the course to the capacity
of what was then Harvard's largest lecture
room. Along with books and people his great
passion was for roses and his garden was
filled with hundreds of bushes which he
tended, often cigar in mouth, with the loving
and respectful care he gave to ballads. Modesty toward himself and affection toward
others were the hallmarks of his character. In
a late letter he wrote, "I should have been
more of a producer, if I had not spent about
half my life in loving people."

In 1880 Child had been a member of the
Harvard faculty thirty-three years and since
1876 the first Professor of English, for which
post he had relinquished the Boylston Pro-
fessorship of Rhetoric and Oratory and with it
most of the drudgery of theme correcting.
Except for a course in advanced composition
and another in eighteenth- and nineteenth-
century literature, both given by Adams S.
Hill, Child was responsible for the English
offering. He needed recruits, and either that

year or the next Kittredge became an obvious
choice for a younger colleague. Kittredge's
reverence and affection for Child were intense
and lasting. Not only did he assist materially
in preparing the last sections of *The English
and Scottish Popular Ballads* for the press, but
he spent untold hours sorting and mounting the
vast collection of Child's letters and manuscript materials now in the Harvard College
Library. His feeling for his master was admirably expressed in his answer to a student who
asked why a passage in Shakespeare was explained in one way by Kittredge and in another
by an editor,"Because *he* did not have Mr. Child
to tell him what was right." The association
was postponed when, after his graduation, Kit-
redge went to Phillips Exeter Academy, where
he taught Latin for five years. In the interim
Child directed Kittredge's private studies, encouraged him to take a year out to study in Ger-
many, where, like Child before him, he attended
courses but did no work toward a degree, and in
1888 brought him back to Harvard. By that time
the Department included Briggs and Barrett
Wendell, and, between then and Child's death
in 1896, George P. Baker, Jefferson B. Fletcher,
Fred N. Robinson, and Charles T. Copeland,
along with a few more transient figures.

In the decade after 1888 Kittredge offered

instruction in Old Norse, Anglo-Saxon, historical English grammar, Middle English, the
metrical romances, Chaucer, Spenser, Shakespeare, the English Bible, Bacon, and Milton.
The list is formidable and no less impressive
when we remember that the teacher had had
the benefit of prior instruction in but few of
the subjects. Kittredge acquired languages
readily — he once said that a reading knowledge of most modern tongues could be picked
up in a hammock during an otherwise idle
summer — and he was a compulsive reader.

The extent of Kittredge's reading is hardly
to be exaggerated. Another Comestor, he read
rapidly and attentively and, despite his phenomenal memory, he obeyed the injunction,
"When found, make a note of." At the age of
fourteen he put together a collection of quotations not found in Bartlett's *Familiar Quotations*, drawing from such authors as Philip
Bailey, John Taylor the Water-Poet, Dante,
William of Wykeham, John Dyer, Shakespeare, George Herbert, Samuel Butler, Robert
Herrick, William of Malmesbury, Thomas
Moore, Byron, Watts, Chatterton, Long-
fellow, Whittier, and Henry Wotton, and from
F. J. Child's first collection of *English and
Scottish Ballads* (a prophetic choice). To
suspect that some of his excerpts came from

volumes of selections is not to detract from
the impressiveness of the list. We miss
Chaucer, but in an essay of the same year
(1874) he quotes from the Canon's Yeoman's
Tale, with a line reference to a nineteenth-
century edition of Tyrwhitt's text. Two years
later he compiled a list of "Words not in
Webster's Unabridged," which included *vom-
iture*, *shard*, *alabareh*, and *hareem* ("probably
a variant of *harem*"). In 1878, his freshman
year, he began the first of a long series of folio
commonplace books, the indexes to which
were ultimately combined in an Index Rerum.
This first volume, with mottoes from Herbert
and Donne, has passages, frequently long and
always out of complete editions, from Ennius,
Thomas Wright's *Songs and Carols*, Defoe's
Political History of the Devil, Walter Mapes,
John Webster, Sir Thomas Browne, Landor
(in more than one place), William of Malmesbury, Massachusetts Colony Records, Jacques
Delille, Cotton's Montaigne, R. H. Wilde of
Augusta (Georgia), John Oldham, the *Chester
Plays*, Skelton, Drayton, Joseph Hall, William
Chappell (three songs with the musical nota-
tions), William Drummond, Donne (at much
greater length than any other poet), Rowlands,
Beaumont and Fletcher, Dekker, Middleton,
Ford, Peele, Jonson, Kyd, Thomas Heywood,

Glapthorne, Tourneur, Marston, Burton, and others. Few students, one suspects, approach their first formal classes in English with such informal preparation. Other undergraduate folios are filled with Greek and Latin, and by the time he was at Exeter he was systematically combing Old French romances. In addition to the commonplace books he had what F. N. Robinson called his Catalogue of Universal Information, a large, twenty-four drawer cabinet filled with indexed and cross-indexed cards from which he could extract references for himself and for other scholars. All these, be it noted, in his own small yet legible hand. He never used a typewriter or in any ordinary sense of the term a research assistant. When we remember that his reading in prose fiction was extensive, and that even from the detective stories he liked so well he snapped up trifles unconsidered by others, it is remarkable that a mere eighty-one years contained the necessary time. For one thing, he kept late hours and had the happy faculty of closing his eyes, sleeping soundly for half an hour and returning refreshed and alert to his books. Reading was to Kittredge as natural a process as breathing.

Kittredge met his last class in 1936 and died

in 1941; those who remember him in action are now well into middle age and are not infrequently asked, "What was Kittredge like?" In the first place, his appearance was one to catch the eye and cling to the memory. There are few more dispiriting sights than the members of a faculty *en masse*. High imagination is required to believe that a huddle of such generally drab and even scruffy people represents a concentration of learning and wisdom. In that company Kittredge stood out like an egret in a flock of cowbirds. He was a little above middle height, spare, and erect until years brought him a scholar's stoop. His striking feature was a full yet ordered beard, all the more evident because he wore it during the interbarbate period, when "Beaver!" could be a challenging game. This beard, as much the subject of wonder and conjecture among his students as any oriflamme, he had grown while still an undergraduate.[5] The reason for the beard was simpler and more human than many of the guesses about it: a tender skin made shaving unpleasant. The beard was at first of a fine brownish red, but it turned early

---

[5] Beards were not a students' thing in the 1880's. In his class (1882) of 181 members, mustaches were common, sideburns, occasionally flowering into burnsides, not uncommon, and there were but ten beards. These facts, as interesting today as at any other time, were garnered from a hasty run through the Class Album.

white, and was so unsullied in its whiteness,
especially on an habitual smoker of cigars,
that some observers maintained that he
washed it with blueing.[6] The mouth was
firm, the nose aquiline, and the blue eyes,
when not hooded, piercing. For reading he
used pince-nez which he manipulated with
gestures of a military precision. The hair on
his head, as if put to rout by the splendor of
the beard, became sparse, a possible explanation of the hat he wore in so many of his
pictures.

Kittredge's fondness for light-colored suits
did not diminish his visibility, nor did his
habit of carrying a cane, a custom which he
abandoned at about the time that age might
have suggested its practical utility. While he
was not above giving the cane a playful flour-
ish, there is no evidence that he used it to
strike at people who were in his way or to
knock off hats unwisely worn inside the
library. He did indeed raise his cane to stop
traffic when crossing a street, but he was never
so oblivious of danger as George Herbert

---

[6] Students' interest in teachers' hair seems often to have reached
the outer limits of fetishism. One group, for example, maintained
that the lank, even, and brown locks of John Livingston Lowes,
Kittredge's student and colleague, were in point of fact a wig, until a
junior Sherlock undermined the theory by seeing Lowes have a
shampoo.

Palmer, who would emerge from the Yard and cross Massachusetts Avenue without lifting his eyes from the ground or breaking the steady patter of his felt-slippered feet.

Cigars, his favorite being the Prince of Monaco, furnished one of the elements in which he lived, and he believed that a good thing should be shared. To doctors' orals he carried a pocketful for himself and the candidate, and when one young scholar left the room after a consumption of five, Kittredge said with emphatic admiration, "That man is a smoker! I move that he be passed." Occasionally a student, too timid or too bold, assayed his first cigar in his first oral and came close to losing more than face. More prudent and perhaps more sentimental non-smokers accepted the cigar as a precious souvenir. His generosity was not limited to students. One of the men who came periodically to dust his books said of him, "Some men will say to you, 'Have a cigar?' Not Kittredge. He puts out a box and says, 'Keep smoking.'" To mention another of life's little pleasures, he liked convivial drinking, but was said to have respected Prohibition to the extent of evading direct contact with bootleggers. He took a cocktail in the old-fashioned way, cold and quick — a sip, a reflective nod, and then an empty glass. In lesser men this method can lead to embarrassment, but if such a misfortune ever happened to Kittredge no one present remembered to tell of it.

Kittredge's fame as a teacher came primarily from his large course in Shakespeare, and, to a degree lesser only because there were fewer students, from his courses in Chaucer and the *Beowulf*. He did not give set lectures, but read aloud with dramatic vigor, pausing for explanatory and interpretative comments which might be as short as a sentence or take as long as fifteen minutes. Except when reading he would stride to and fro across the platform, a truly peripatetic teacher. His comments were clear and beautifully expressed, touched on every aspect of the text, and explained what the author meant to himself and to his original audience. A phenomenal memory allowed him to recall in paraphrase or quotation the context around a word or phrase given in a question or to teach the *Beowulf* from an unmarked text. He did not ignore the new corn which comes out of old fields, but he had little part in attempts to state what an early author might have had in mind had he known what he could not know. Naturally enough he talked about words and about their histories, but his method was not philological, in the senselessly opprobrious sense of that word. He made his students realize that effort was required to comprehend Chaucer or Shakespeare and he made most of them feel that the effort was pleasant. The exposition was essentially dramatic, in that there was a steady and uninhibited interplay between the poet and the teacher, and neither suffered in the process. It was not Kittredge's fault if the interplay did not include the students as well. He constantly stopped to invite, indeed demand questions, and could become fretful if they were not forthcoming.

Other words than "fretful" have been applied to Kittredge's demeanor in the classroom, and there were undoubtedly some who found it oppressive. His concept of decorous behavior was offensive to the few who could smell permissiveness afar, and his insistence that students conform to his ideal caused him to be called a martinet. He sometimes induced conformity by explosions of wrath so spectacular as to be unforgettable and thereby multiplied in tradition. Actually, outbursts were rare and certainly not brought on by every temptation. By comparison with his classmate and colleague, Charles Townsend Copeland, he had no more gall than a dove. His rages were so irregular and sometimes seemed so staged, that there were those who held that he had in his texts such personal directions as "Stir up the animals," or "Exit, pursued by a tantrum." Although attractive, the theory is probably untenable. Certain things affronted his sense of fitness. To him the wearing of a hat in the classroom, or indeed the library, approached sacrilege, and to do so usually received due attention, as did the reading of newspapers during the class hour. Coughing distracted him and his efforts to suppress it were often accompanied by the somewhat self-righteous statement that this was a pernicious habit which he had conquered years since. On the other hand, he was genial with the somnolent and, unlike Copeland, rarely took offense at latecomers who seated themselves quietly in the back of the classroom. Indeed, he sometimes welcomed the tardy by quoting "While the lamp holds out to burn . . ." Failure to elicit any response to a request for questions might lead him to a class list, direct questions to individuals, and perhaps a slaughter of the innocent. Here his terrible patience was often more disconcerting than anger. Sensitive students were occasionally hurt by this public invasion of their intellectual privacy, but, human nature being the sorry thing it is, the rest of the class was more delighted than purged. His rare departures usually came when no one would admit knowing what to him was some simple and necessary fact, and he urged the class to use the remainder of the hour to gain the information. At least once he shepherded the group into Widener Library to give them a fair start. The overwhelming majority accepted the rules, which they had known about before they elected the course, and were more disappointed than not if at the end of the year their teacher could wear white gloves. It can be, and is, argued that ignorance, recalcitrance, and stupidity are better ignored, but that was not always Kittredge's way. He once said, "I am willing to make a fool of myself for your benefit, and it seems only fair that I should make fools of you now and then for the same purpose." He had, in truth, a strong temper which he could not or would not always control, and which he explained as inseparable from the temperament which his once red hair made manifest. If on reflection he decided that he had lost it unworthily, he made a handsome and usually satisfying apology.

In his small courses, such as those on ballads or romances, Kittredge's method was anything but dramatic. Whereas in the larger groups his comments, even after many years, seemed spontaneous, associative, and immediate, here he adhered closely to carefully prepared notes, replete with bibliographical references. When he expanded, as in matters of theory, he would shut his eyes and the effect of the quiet voice emerging from the immobile beard had a trancelike effect. One could not choose but to believe. He met his graduate courses throughout the year, his own lectures in the first term and the presentation of reports in the second. The papers were given at evening meetings in his house on Hilliard Street. Although he rarely interrupted the speaker, and indeed usually gave an appearance of quiet and contented slumber, his criticism was full, incisive, helpful, and never harsh or niggling. The hour or two of general and smoky conversation which concluded the sessions gave the participants a feeling of friendly contact, knowing and being known, which they seldom enjoyed with other teachers. Kittredge, contrary to a somewhat general impression, was altogether approachable. He did not, to be sure, regard the library as a place for informal interviews nor did he stop on the street for a bit of chitchat. A student once reported, "I met Mr. Kittredge on Massachusetts Avenue today and he was most gracious." "What did he say to you?" "He didn't say anything, but the way he walked by me was very courteous." If anyone who had reason to consult Kittredge took the trouble to telephone him, he invariably was given a prompt appointment and, the appointment kept, he was never made to feel hurried or that he was infringing on the time of a great and busy man.

He took infinite pains with the theses prepared under his direction and his interest continued long after the degree was received. His letter files are full of requests for suggestions on revision and assistance toward publication, sometimes a quarter of a century after the thesis had been completed. He always did what he could, even when importunity must have tried his patience. For Kittredge to direct a dissertation was to accept a lifelong assignment.

Teaching for Kittredge was not a skill that could be induced by precept or training, and he rejected all opportunities to analyze his own methods for the benefit of others. Indignation was his only response to a questionnaire which asked, among other things, how much time he spent in preparation for an hour in the classroom, and when asked for a brief statement as to how he taught, he replied briefly enough, "That's a question that I'm quite unable to answer." On another occasion he said that a teacher requires only three things, "A knowledge of his subject, adequate vocal cords, and students." He once told a class, "I can't teach you anything, but there is nothing under God's heaven you can't learn."

During almost fifty years oral examinations in the Division of Modern Languages and Kittredge were identical. He rarely missed an oral, either for undergraduate honors or for the doctor's degree, his participation was continual and lively, and he never complained of a crushing burden. His obvious enjoyment of orals may have made him suspect among his more reluctant colleagues, but it was a comfort and joy to the insecure and apprehensive victim. He was a skilled and imaginative examiner, almost always in the candidate's corner or, to change the figure, his champion in the lists. His questions were short, pointed, and clear, and he aided other examiners to make theirs the same, not always perhaps to their gratification. "What Professor Blank wants to know, if I understand him, is . . ." He was especially adept at straightening out the dire clues in the hour on Germanic linguistics which was the curtain-

raiser under the old system. In the discussion
which determined the candidate's fate Kittredge, either because he presided, which as
Chairman of the Division he ordinarily did, or
by seating himself strategically, had the last
word. If the judgments were favorable, he
said little, but if the tide seemed to be going
against the candidate, he spoke at length and
if necessary often, always in favor of a pass.
Usually he and the candidate won, either by
eloquence, by cajolery, or by prolonging the
discussion half an hour or more past lunch-
time. Some held that this was not so much
sheer philanthropy as a distaste for breaking
unpleasant news. Once he did leave Warren
House through a window rather than face a
failed man. If there were those who felt that
Kittredge's soft-heartedness defeated justice
and lowered the degree, this opinion was not
common among graduate students.

The story goes that Kittredge was asked
why he never took a doctor's degree and that
he replied, "Who would have examined me?"
Here, unfriends said, is plain proof of ar-
rogance, but the history of the PhD in English
at Harvard makes the proof lame, even if the
anecdote be true. The first doctor's degree in
English was given in 1876 and the next in
1888, the year in which Kittredge joined the

minuscule Department. From the outset he was an examiner and a teacher of courses which graduate students took. The answer, if given at all, refers to the resources of the Department and not to the speaker's assumption of superiority. Kittredge in truth was a shy and modest man. He was decisive, which may have made him appear dogmatic, and he was rarely wrong in matters of fact, which could make people who had differed find him overbearing. Accuracy was a passion with him, yet one which could be expressed with humor, as a pair of examples may suggest. One aspect of his showmanship was his ability to talk himself out of the classroom and utter his last word with his hand on the doorknob and the bell above beginning to toll. To do this even Kittredge had to keep track of time, and one morning he borrowed a watch from a student in the front row. He evidently felt that some explanation was necessary and so said, "I am not requesting the loan because I do not own a watch. In fact, I own two watches. One is now at the jeweler's and the other was taken from my house twenty-three years ago." Again, when a female candidate had withdrawn from her oral, someone asked idly, "How old do you suppose she is?" and another gave the unchivalric and now dated reply, "She must be as old as King Tut." Kittredge looked at the record and settled the matter, "Eleven years older."

No arrogant dogmatist could have had as many friends as Kittredge did or been a cherished member of so many clubs. He loved to fold, or rather stretch out, his legs and have his talk. Taste or convention tended to limit his social hours to masculine society, and his friends were academics and business or professional men with informed tastes in books and history. Because he was an orthodox Congregationalist and a conservative in politics he might not have been at ease with voluble atheists and levellers, but there were Unitarians, perhaps some who were even freer thinkers, and liberals verging discreetly upon radicalism, among his friends. In a series of essays of 1874 he had listed the three great American statesmen of the nineteenth century as Henry Clay, Daniel Webster, and Charles Sumner, had given some thought to extending the death penalty as an extreme measure to reduce petty crime, and could see that on rare occasions, such as the Chicago Fire, Vigilance Committee Law and even Lynch Law "seem almost absolutely necessary." The Whig-Republican tradition is clear enough, but in the same papers he wrote in favor of Woman's

Suffrage, took a philosophical view of the election of a Democratic governor of Massachusetts, and maintained with spirit that "Aristocracy is nonsense." An essay entitled "How Shall I Earn a Living," contained no reference to teaching, and another, "Qualities of a Good Business Man," suggests that a business or professional man must watch his step to keep out of jail. Whatever tenets the tree held over from the twig, Kittredge was not a political professor and never let personal convictions about current events color his teaching.

Kittredge had no patience with scholarly fads and whimsies and attacked them with ridicule as often as with reason. When petrified verse was being found in Shakespeare's prose, he could find it in Milton's prose, not too unlikely a source, and also in modern detective stories. He aided the etymological mythologizers by showing that their own names, properly handled, gave evidence of divine origin. Anagrams and cryptograms were one of his favorite sports; once he proved that the menu for a certain dinner was composed by Keats with an assist from Marlowe. In the field of topical allusions he demonstrated at length and with a wealth of historical details that *Romeo and Juliet* is

based on the murder of Sir Thomas Overbury.
The only difficulty lay in the date of the play
(1595-1596) and that of the murder (1613),
but Kittredge was convinced that this trifle
would be cleared up as readily as many of the
discrepancies found in similar interpretations.
He antedated the full flowering of sexual
symbolism, which is rather a pity, though his
sense of taste might well have kept him from
expounding "tongues in trees, books in the
running brooks, Sermons in stones and" sex
"in every thing," or any of a hundred thousand
other vulnerable lines. Here it may be noted
that although Kittredge shared the reticences
of his breed and generation, he was no prude.
He told and enjoyed anecdotes of the kind
once called off-color, but, and this again was
of his generation, his stories had a scatological
rather than a sexual point. In teaching
Chaucer he read more of the fabliaux than was
common at the time, and he defended Chaucer
against those, such as the American critic and
statesman Theodore Roosevelt, who accused
the poet of immorality. For Kittredge what
Chaucer wrote was anything but pornography,
which he once defined in an apparently off-
hand classroom comment as "literature written
specifically for the excessive, improper, im-
moral, and inopportune arousal of passion."

Three things determined Kittredge's eminence in his world: his personality, his learning, and the fact that he came into academic life at a time when American graduate study in the modern languages and literatures was just entering its first great cycle. Before he died he saw perceptible changes in emphasis and methods, but there is no evidence that he lamented the passing of a brave old world. His interests were wide and he encouraged others to widen their own, a fact made clear by the variety of doctoral dissertations which he directed. He believed that students of modern literature should know the classics and that students of English literature should be familiar with the development of the English language, and one suspects that he found it difficult to think that there could be general disagreement on those points. What endeared him to his students was not so much his erudition as his willingness to share it, his infinite patience with their first attempts at scholarship, and his aid in furthering their careers. If he was aware of personal conflict between research and teaching, it was resolved in favor of teaching. His writings are a noble monument, and yet he could have varied Child's remark, "I should have been more of a producer, if I had not spent about half my life in helping people."

PREFACE

THE six lectures that compose this volume were delivered at the Johns Hopkins University in April and May, 1914, being the nineteenth course of lectures on Poetry on the Percy Turnbull Memorial Foundation. They are printed as delivered, except for such slight emendations as naturally suggest themselves when one prepares a manuscript for the press. Since the plan of the book excludes footnotes, I wish to make the fullest kind of general acknowledgment to Chaucerian scholars in both hemispheres for the help which their published writings have afforded me. To the founders of the lectureship, and to my friends and colleagues in Baltimore, I am deeply indebted for their cordial expressions of interest and their delightful hospitality.

CAMBRIDGE, January 22, 1915.

CHAUCER AND HIS POETRY

CHAUCER AND HIS POETRY

I

THE MAN AND HIS TIMES

THERE is no great harm in the air of patronage with which our times, in their self-satisfied enlightenment, address the great who were of old; but we do use droll adjectives! If these great ancients show the simplicity of perfect art, we call them *naïf*, particularly when their irony eludes us; if they tickle our fancy, they are *quaint*; if we find them altogether satisfactory, both in form and substance, we adorn them with the epithet *modern*, which we somehow think is a superlative of eminence. *Naïf, quaint, modern,*—a singular vocabulary! Add *convincing*, and the critic has done his best, or his worst.

For it is we that are naïf; quaintness is incompatible with art; and as for modernity, what we mistake for that, is the everlasting truth, the enduring quality that consists in conformity to changeless human nature. " The ancients," said a wise man, "never understood that they were ancients."

Chaucer lived in the middle ages, in the last sixty years, or thereabout, of the fourteenth century; but he is the most modern of English poets, and one of the most popular. This is not a paradox; it is the sober, unrhetorical statement of a truism. For he knew life and loved it, and his specialty was mankind as it was, and is. Besides, his age was vastly like our own, in everything but costume and "the outward habit of encounter." The fourteenth century seems less remote than the eighteenth; Geoffrey Chaucer is nearer to us than Alexander Pope.

It was an age of intense activity, — a singularly "modern" time. One is tempted to assert that all the problems which vex the world to-day, either sprang into existence or made themselves especially troublesome in the sixty years of Chaucer's life. For there is scarcely a political or social catchword of the present (even "feminism," as I hope to show in due season) which does not fit the fourteenth century.

Labor gave trouble in a dozen ways. The Black Death cut down the supply of farm-hands throughout the country. Those who were left, once little better than slaves, asserted themselves in a manner that terrified vested interests and prompted futile legislation. France was convulsed by the savage turmoil of the Jacquerie. In England there were the uprisings of Wat Tyler, John Ball, and Jack Straw, partly a revolt against unjust taxation and tyrant landlords, and partly, especially in London, an assault upon the Flemings, who had been imported by Edward III to establish the manufacture of cloth, and of whom native workmen were insanely jealous. Theories of government that men had held divine were boldly challenged, "antiquity forgot, custom not known." Anarchy borrowed the language of democracy; and the great order of the ages was to begin anew. Gower is our witness for the panic of conservatives in the face of the mob, which had little humor, but much rudimentary logic, and was eager to come by its own.

The art of war was undergoing a profound and alarming change. Chivalry, discredited as a fighting method — for the man-at-arms on foot had forced back the mounted knight — displayed itself all the more splendidly as a social system, decked with fine phrases and brilliant pageantry.

The Eastern Question took on a strangely modern aspect. In 1343 the Turk first got a foothold in Europe, and twenty years later began the meteoric career of Tamerlane, infinitely prophetic of barbarous possibilities from the Orient.

The revolt against the Pope, which led to the complicated movement known as the Reformation, began in the fourteenth century, with Wyclif in England and John Huss in Bohemia. There was a violent reaction in the period following, but in Chaucer's lifetime the Lollard agitation, which involved the most startling radicalism, gained immense headway. With the political leaders of this party Chaucer was on terms of intimate friendship, though there is no evidence that he adopted any of their heresies. The questions at issue seem, at first sight, remote enough. In fact, however, they concerned that vital matter, the relation between Church and State, which, under one or another guise, is still momentous in European politics.

The Revival of Learning also falls in Chaucer's century. Petrarch and Boccaccio were his contemporaries; to both he was indebted, to the latter in larger measure than to any poet but Ovid. The interest in education was wide-spread. A whole chain of universities, from Cracow to Saint Andrews, was established between 1340 and 1410.

Imperialism was never a more vital question than at this time. The armed assertion of Edward's claim to the crown of France, the war of Richard II in Ireland, and the attempt of John of Gaunt to seize the kingdom of Castile, show how far-reaching this movement was.

One can even see a forecast of the gold and silver question. Edward's gold nobles became immediately famous. They were readily accepted by foreign merchants everywhere, as sovereigns pass current to-day. The failure of two great Florentine banking houses, the Bardi and the Peruzzi, in 1345, when Chaucer was a boy, does not sound particularly mediæval. King Edward, by the way, owed them a million and a half of gold florins — a sum which I shall not venture to compute in modern values.

Many such details might be accumulated; but I have said enough to indicate that Chaucer was born in a time of great religious and political and literary activity, not so much at the end of the middle ages as at the beginning of the modern world.

It is vastly fortunate that Chaucer was born high enough in the social scale not to need holy orders as a means of escape from cramping circumstances. Otherwise, a great poet would have been spoiled to make an indifferent parson. He would still have been a poet, and patrons would not have failed him, but he could not have comprehended the world, or "had his life in his time." It is equally fortunate that Chaucer was not born an aristocrat; for then he would not have understood the lower orders, but would have lived and died the poet of chivalric love. We might have had the Troilus, but we should lack the Canterbury Tales.

Happy the destiny that plunged Chaucer into public business, and the practical talents that

brought him so many occupations in such great
variety! His family was of the burgher class,
but it had some kind of court connections or in-
fluence, so that he became page to the Countess
of Ulster, and was afterwards attached to the
royal household. All his life he had public employment. He served in the army, and was taken
prisoner and ransomed. He was Controller of
the Customs, Clerk of the King's Works (or Commissioner of Buildings), Commissioner of what
we should now call the Thames Conservancy,
and M. P. for the County of Kent. At least
seven times he went abroad on diplomatic business, — to France, to Italy, and to Flanders. His
missions were very various: they involved questions of war, of commerce, and of the king's marriage, with other negotiations of which we know
only that they were secret. As courtier, officeholder, soldier, ambassador, legislator, burgher
of London, Chaucer knew everybody that was
worth knowing, high or low. It is hard to imagine a career so thoroughly adapted to fit him
for the great task for which he came into the
world. No man can have had a broader or more
intimate acquaintance with the life of the time.
All this did not make him a poet, for genius comes
only by the grace of God; but it trained him for
the appointed application of his powers —which
was, that he should record the age, in its habit as

it lived, with every significant detail of its "form
and pressure."

Finally, — and this was of prime importance,
— Chaucer was born in London. His native dialect was that which was to become, in the natural course of events, the English of literature.
And it was a critical moment, when nothing was
needed to determine the tendency but a poet of
commanding genius. Chaucer did not make the
English language. His service was to write the
Midland dialect with an ease, a polish, and a regularity which commanded immediate and unanimous admiration, and to use it as the vehicle for
first-rate poetry. Nothing more was needed.
Those who came after him had now an accepted
standard. Lydgate, in his fumbling fashion, tries
to express this great fact, which everybody ap-
preciated, when he says of Chaucer, "Dante in
English himself doth so express." He means,
presumably, that Chaucer's relation to the best
English was that of Dante to the best Italian.

The chief difference between the fourteenth
century and our own, in intellectual matters, lies,
I think, in a different attitude toward specializa-
tion. Our tendency is to exhaust one subject, if
we can, and ignore the rest; theirs was to aspire
to an encyclopædic grasp of the universe. Other
points of contrast are usually emphasized. We
hear, for instance, that our times are blessed

with a critical or questioning spirit, whereas our mediæval ancestors believed what they were told, with blind faith. This, however, is at best a very crude antithesis and it has no merit whatever when applied to Chaucer's lifetime. Then, if ever, the spirit of radicalism was abroad in the land. To describe as an era of dumb submissiveness the age of Wyclif, and John Huss, and the Great Schism, of the Jacquerie in France and Tyler and Ball in England, is to read both literature and history with one's eyes shut. Equally fallacious is the alleged contrast as to what is called the scientific temper, with its appendage the inductive method. We have shifted our ground, perhaps, in some particulars, but we have not much changed our mental habits. We are still led by generalities, quite as much as by experience, though we may apply them rather to politics and the social system than to the natural sciences. And even there, one must not be too confident of an actualized millennium now, or too incredulous of enlightenment then. Empiricism was the sole guide, in practice, of the alchemical brethren to whom the Canon's Yeoman had attached himself. It was not the calm precepts of placid deduction that scattered their gold, and blew up their laboratories, and poisoned them with the fumes of sulphur and antimony.

What strikes me, therefore, when I try to comprehend the second half of the fourteenth century, is not the strangeness, but the familiarity. It was a scambling and unquiet time, when nobody was at rest but the dead. In a word, it was a good age to live in, and so Chaucer found it. But, as I have said, it differed from our own in one regard:—the man of intellect read everything he could lay his hands on; he did not confine his interests to his specialty, even if he had one.

Now Chaucer's specialty was mankind. It is not surprising, therefore, that his works show great variety. "Learned Chaucer" people used to call him, when learning was a title of honor; and though the term sounds stilted, and has been much assailed of late, as lacking in appropriateness, it was not ill-chosen. Of course, Chaucer was not accurate; but accuracy concerns scholarship rather than learning, and the distinction is fundamental. Walter Burley confused Epaminondas with Epimenides, Socrates with Isocrates, Xenophanes with Xenophon, and *lauriger Horatius* with Horatius Pulvillus. Titus Livius appears in his pages as "historian and writer of tragedies," by amalgamation, one sees, with Livius Andronicus. Yet Burley was a man of learning and a professional teacher, engaged, at the moment of blundering, in the compilation of a biographical text-book for college students.

What concerns us, then, is not the venial lapses
of Chaucer in his details, but the wide sweep of
his intellectual interests, and the variety of his
performance. His specialty was mankind, and
his writings are almost conterminous with human interests, if we omit politics and diplomacy,
which were his profession. Science is represented
by the Astrolabe, high philosophy by Boethius,
practical ethics by the Melibee, everyday theology by the Tale of the Parson. Society, in all its
aspects, is the continual theme of Chaucer's
verse.

Paradoxical as it seems to us, Chaucer must
have ranked high as a religious writer. Not to
speak of his legends, he put forth his A B C, an
elaborate prayer to the Virgin, advancing through
all the letters of the alphabet. He translated a
famous work of mortification, Innocent on the
Wretched Condition of Mankind, and a famous
homily upon the Magdalen, ascribed to Origen.
Finally, he closed his great survey of human life
in the Canterbury Tales with a practical treatise
on Penitence and the Seven Deadly Sins, which
he appropriately assigned to the good priest, the
poor but learned parson of a town. Chaucer's
knowledge of theology, and his interest in some
of its highest problems, are evinced in countless
passages, long and short, in his poetical works.

As to science, I have mentioned the Astrolabe.

Astrology, which implies astronomy, was at his fingers' ends. How far he credited its doctrines, one is quite at a loss to determine. Astronomy, however, was only one of the scientific subjects that interested him. Medicine was much better known to him than to his learned editors, as Mr. Lowes has recently proved. The physiological ætiology of dreams, as well as their possible significance, was a subject to which he returned again and again. His acquaintance with alchemy was the wonder of the adepts of the seventeenth century. Elias Ashmole thought that Chaucer was himself a disciple, a spagyric student, a pyrotechnist, a philosopher by the fire. And Ashmole was nearer right than those of us who idly fancy that the poet worked up the terms of the art in a perfunctory fashion, *ad hoc*, for the sake of a rollicking satire. This is much like the ingenious suggestion of an eminent scholar that Chaucer had read a few romances in order to parody them in Sir Thopas.

An eccentric notion prevails among the ignorant revilers of mediævalism that the authors of those times were unchastened by line or precept. Lawless, amorphous, chaotic — such are the adjectives to which our ears are habituated. These are wild shots. Never, I suppose, was the principle of law and order in literature more dominant than in the middle ages. Schematism held

undisputed sway in the schools. Rules were accepted as if they came from heaven. Flowers of
rhetoric were culled, classified, labelled, and
stored up in the herbarium. Law, not license,
was the watchword of the mediæval writer. The
struggle of any original genius was not to discover fetters, but to break them, or rather, to
apply to his inspired use the consecrated formulas, without being cramped or paralyzed.

That Chaucer was no untaught phenomenon,
but had studied rhetoric to good purpose, should
be obvious to the most precipitate of readers,
even if that masterpiece of *eloquentia*, the Tale
of the Man of Law, had not come down to us.
Again and again he mentions the formalities of
his art, now in his own person, now through the
medium of some fictitious character. It is a cardinal principle, he tells us, that the style should
be appropriate to the subject: "the wordes mote
be cosyn to the dede."[1] The knight of the brazen
horse, in the Squire's Tale, made his address of
presentation in due form, "withouten vyce of
syllable or of lettre," in the high style, which the
narrator cannot imitate, and with bearing, gestures, and behavior that suited his words, in
accordance with the precepts of oratory, or "art
of speech."[2] The Franklin, who regrets his own
son's lack of culture, praises the Squire for his

---

[1] Canterbury Tales, A. 741-742; cf. H. 207-208.   [2] F. 99-109.

eloquence, using the term in its technical meaning of elegance and elevation of phrase, the
Latin *eloquentia*. So impressed, indeed, is the
worthy vavasour that he disclaims all knowledge of "colors of rhetoric" (another technical
term) when he begins his own story, on the Host's
impatient demand.[1] "High style" is a term
well known to Harry Bailly, who, as Chaucer expressly informs us, was wise and well-taught.[2]
He begs the Clerk to keep such diction for letters
meant for royalty.[3] This same Clerk, indeed, is
a literary critic. He even ventures a modest censure on Petrarch's Proem to Griselda, which
seems to him "a thing impertinent," save that
it might help to get a hearing for the novel —
"save that he wol conveyen his matere."[4]

Several of Chaucer's references to things rhetorical are in his characteristic deprecatory manner. It is certain, however, that he often embel-
lished his writing, consciously and deliberately,
with "flowers" or "colors." Noteworthy, for
instance, is his frequent use of apostrophe, — not
casually, but with very definite purpose. Sometimes he is serious; sometimes, as in the tale of
the Nun's Priest, the effect is that of parody.
This tale, by the way, would well repay the study
of a technical rhetorician. It is, in form, an exemplum, or preacher's illustrative anecdote, enor-

---

[1] F. 673-728.   [2] A. 755.   [3] E. 16-20.   [4] E. 41-55.

mously developed until it swallows up the sermon.
But it is also — and this is the significant thing
— a mock heroic poem, perfectly constructed,
and finished to the last detail. Every trick of
style which the schools taught is utilized for
comic effect. It is here, we remember, that Geoffrey de Vinsauf is apostrophized as "dere maister
sovereyn," with an ironical aspiration to his
learning and sententiousness, and a particular encomium on his invective against the Friday that
was fatal to Richard of the Lion Heart.

Schematism is not beauty, but it is certainly not
license. Chaucer is more than once impelled to
apologize for disregarding that regularity of arrangement which his readers expected. With
his usual irony, of the Socratic sort, he ascribes
this breach of decorum to his feeble intellect. So,
in the person of the Monk, he begs pardon for
transgressing chronology in the order of the
"tragedies."[1] More amusing is the example in the
general Prologue, where pardon is asked, on the
plea of a "short wit," for letting the pilgrims tell
their tales without due heed to social precedence.[2]
Yet, after all, the Knight begins the series, not
by appointment, but by the judgment of the
lots, which prove more deferential to rank and
station than the poet himself. Another apology
for lack of method comes from the Canon's

<hr>

[1] B. 3174–3180.   [2] A. 743–746.

Yeoman, when he expounds the mysteries of alchemy. "He is an ignorant man," he avers, "and that must be his excuse for disorder in the rehearsal of things pertaining to the spagyric art."[1] His whole lecture, in truth, is made riotously comic by haphazard enumeration. Ingredients, utensils, processes, and miscellaneous terms are jumbled together in a mad and merry dance of technicalities: — verdigris, borax, vials, crucibles, and alembics, the rubification of water, bull's gall, arsenic and brimstone, valerian and lunary, lamps, furnaces, albification of water, lime, chalk, the white of eggs, waxed bags, saltpeter, wood and coal fires, sal tartar and alkali, alum, glass and yeast, imbibing, citrinization, ingots, test-tubes, and many more!

The passage is a veritable Aristophanic *pnigos*, — only it is not (like that) an operatic *tour de force*. The whole tumultuous farrago is the excited Yeoman's "unpacking his heart with words." The terms are not half understood by him — though he feels an ignorant man's pride in displaying so prodigious a vocabulary — and they are quite unintelligible to the pilgrims. The hopelessness of mastering such a jargon is, to them, the best proof that the philosopher's stone is beyond the reach of human effort.

Every work of Chaucer's is referable to some

[1] G. 784–789.

definite literary category which was recognized as such by his educated contemporaries. Thus we have the legend of a saint, in the Life of Saint Cecilia (afterward allotted, without revision, to the Second Nun); a miracle of the Virgin, in the tale of the martyred little boy, certainly written expressly for the Prioress, and exquisitely attuned to her character; a romantic legend, in the story of Constance (told by the Man of Law), full of fabulous materials, but subdued by its edifying purpose to a consistent impression of melancholy devoutness. Here should be mentioned the Legend of the Saints of Cupid (otherwise called Good Women), in which, in accordance with the mediæval convention equating Love's service with our duty toward God, the lives of Cleopatra, Dido, Phyllis, Medea, and the rest are collected, partly from Ovid's Heroides, into a strange reflex of the Legenda Aurea. There is the love-vision — modified in various ways and applied to divers ends — in the Book of the Duchess, the Parliament of Fowls, the House of Fame, and the Prologue to the Legend of Good Women. We have also long romances: — the pure romance of adventure, in the Squire's Tale, and, by way of boisterous and affectionate parody, in Sir Thopas; the Italianate romance, in Palamon and Arcite; the same, developed into a psychological novel, in the Troilus. Of the shorter

forms of narrative, there is every variety, — the
episodical romance, in the Wife's Tale; the lay
of Britain, in the Franklin's; the tragedy, ancient
and modern, in the Tale of the Monk. Fabliaux
abound, — the purely jocose, as told by the
Reeve and the Miller; the jocose with clever in-
trigue and a touch of satire, in the Shipman's
Tale; the satiric wonder-story, in the Friar's
Tale; and the gross anecdote expanded and
transmuted into an exquisite satire, in the Sumner's. Finally, there is what may well pass for
a contemporary anecdote, in the tricks of the
alchemist as detailed by the Canon's Yeoman.

In his best work Chaucer shows all the qualities which, in modern authors, are accounted
"regular" or "classical," or whatever the fashionable epithet may be. His verse, though full of
variety, is always in exquisite tune. There never
was a better or more finished metrician. His
sense of rhythm, indeed, is quite extraordinary,
even for a poet. The heroic couplet, which he
introduced into our language, he handles with
a mastery that none but Dryden has ever
approached. The Troilus stanza, likewise his in-
vention, is, as he employs it, a perfect medium
of expression, — alike for narrative, for description, for reflection, and (what is most remarkable)
for easy and graceful dialogue. His diction has
an elegant simplicity which produces, in its con-

summate art, the deceptive effect of artlessness. It achieves decorum without apparent effort and with no suggestion of formality. Its freedom from puns, conceits, jingles, and antithetic affectations moved the admiration of Dryden, who found in Chaucer a "continence," so he calls it, "which is practised by few writers, and scarcely by any of the ancients, excepting Virgil and Horace."

Dryden, as a matter of course, could not rid himself of the queer notion that Chaucer "lived in the dawning of our language," and he inferred, with a singular kind of logic (to which some recent critics are likewise prone) that the poet's vocabulary must somehow be rude and inchoate. "The words," he says, "are given up [by me] as a post not to be defended in our poet, because he wanted the modern art of fortifying." This dictum rests, in the last analysis, on the odd assumption that obsoleteness and crudity are one and the same thing. Dryden, I fancy, knew better; but he was arguing Chaucer's case before a prejudiced jury, and he felt the wisdom of waiving an unessential point that it was dangerous to press. Besides, he was at a disadvantage from his utter ignorance of Chaucer's grammar, and therefore of his metre, which he compared to the "rude sweetness of a Scotch tune." Yet he says enough to show, if one attends, that he recognized the excellence of Chaucer's style—its force, its finished ease, its simplicity, and its purity of idiom.

Conciseness is another of Chaucer's "classical" virtues. The condensation of Boccaccio's Teseide into the Knight's Tale is a truly marvellous performance. Dryden saw this quality, but could not free himself from the prejudices of his age, and leaves upon our minds the impression— intentionally or unintentionally — that frequent excision is necessary to reduce the Canterbury Tales to modern standards of proportion and good judgment. In fact, however, Dryden has expanded the text materially in all his versions, — about ten per cent in Palamon and Arcite, and about one-third in the Cock and Fox and the Wife of Bath's Tale, while he has frankly increased the Character of a Good Parson to nearly three times its original length. The artistic economy of Chaucer, even in descriptive passages, where decoration would be excusable, goes quite beyond all Dryden's power of self-control. Nor can the modern master refrain from interpolating allusions and reflections. They are apt and pointed, I admit, but they tend to dissipate the attention, which Chaucer's art keeps focussed on the thing itself. So, for instance, in the famous description of the Temple of Mars. One brief comparison will suffice to illustrate the difference: —

The dore was al of adamant eterne,
Yclenched overthwart and endelong
With iren tough; and for to make it strong,
Every pyler, the temple to sustene,
Was tonne greet, of iren bright and shene.[1]

The gate was adamant, eternal frame,
Which, hewed by Mars himself, from Indian quarries
    came,
The labor of a god; and all along
Tough iron plates were clenched, to make it strong.
A tun about was every pillar there, —
A polished mirror shone not half so clear.[2]

Chaucer's sense of proportion is quite as remarkable as his skill in construction and his artistic economy. Such a story as the Pardoner's Tale is, in all these ways, absolutely perfect. Observe, in particular, the extraordinary rapidity of the resolution after the climax. Two of the rioters guard the treasure, while the third, the youngest, goes to town for food and drink. They plot to kill him on his return. He, for his part, plans the death of the two as he rides along, and he brings back three leather bottles of wine, two poisoned. Thus we reach the acme of the climax, which, in this wonderful story, is a point of extreme suspense, with crisscross ironies of circumstance comparable to those at the end of Hamlet. Mark, now, the quiet, rapid, relentless march of the resolution: — ten verses, with a six-line epilogue:

[1] Knight's Tale, 1990–1994.   [2] Palamon and Arcite, 1164–1169.

What nedeth it to sermone of it moore?
For right as they hadde cast his deeth bifoore,
Right so they han hym slayn, and that anon.
And whan that this was doon, thus spak that oon:
"Now lat us sitte and drynke, and make us merie,
And afterward we wol his body berie."
And with that word it happed hym, par cas,
To take the botel ther the poyson was,
And drank, and yaf his felawe drynke also,
For which anon they storven bothe two.

But certes, I suppose that Avycen
Wroot nevere in no canon, ne in no fen,
Mo wonder signes of empoisonyng
Than hadde thise wrecches two, er hir endyng.
Thus ended been thise homycides two,
And eek the false empoysonere also.

In studying the structure and proportions of
this matchless short-story, we must, of course,
disregard the long preachment against drink,
dicing, and oaths. The whole tale, as it lies before us, is one of the Pardoner's sermons, consist-
ing of text ("the love of money is the root of all
evil"), brief introduction, illustrative anecdote
(or *exemplum*), and application. The exemplum
alone is narrative, and this is readily isolated.
The rest is admirable in its own way, and quite
amazing in its verisimilitude. The Pardoner is
an abandoned wretch, but he is truly a "noble
ecclesiast." The cynical frankness of his confession in the prologue, contrasted with the eloquence
and apparent earnestness of the sermon, and

with the beauty and impressiveness of the exemplum he uses, produces a psychological situation of intolerable stress and strain.

His cynicism suddenly abandons him, and —
in a moment, in the twinkling of an eye — he
becomes a changed man, reverting to the days
before he lost his soul. Then, on the instant, he
recovers his reckless bearing, and seems to be
past the crisis. But there is an explosion, after
all. Emotional forces like these cannot be quietly dissipated. There comes the quarrel with
the Host, and only the Knight can restore peace.

Chaucer's swiftness in the resolution has given
rise to strange comments. Mr. Lounsbury, for
instance, in speaking of the Book of the Duchess
and the Parliament of Fowls, remarks that in
both "the ending is so abrupt that it gives the
impression that the author left off, not because
he had got through with what he started out to
say, but because he was too tired to go on. There
is a sense of incompleteness about the two poems
which detracts from their perfection as works of
art." [1] I am not concerned to defend the Parliament, which has met with quite as much appreciation as it deserves. The conclusion, however,
as well as that of the Duchess, is quite perfect,
even masterly. In one case the dreamer is roused
by the din that the birds make, in the other by

[1] Studies in Chaucer, III, 320.

the striking of the tower-clock. In both, the vision is finished, and the fancied abruptness is merely the instantaneous passage from sleep to waking. What more there was to say, I cannot imagine.

The general impression is that mediæval writers are digressive — that they can seldom resist the lure of any chance idea, no matter how far afield it strays, particularly when such vagrancy leads them into learned regions. This impression has, with the general run of critics, hardened into a fixed idea. Whenever a poet ventures a classical or a scientific allusion, he is accused of pedantry, of a childish fondness for "showing off." Neither the interest of the digression nor the pertinency of the allusion is taken into account.

The truth is, that mediæval writers are not, in general, more prone to digression than those of other periods. Some digress, and some do not, precisely as in modern times. The prevalent notion admits of an easy diagnosis. It comes, in the first place, from the mediæval habit of inserting illustrative stories. Frequently an author, instead of making a touch-and-go allusion, will pause to tell the tale. So, for example, with the dream-anecdotes of Chanticleer, and with Midas' Ears in the Wife's romance of the Loathly Lady. This habit, however, is not due to lack of method. The examples are almost always pertinent, and their insertion is a part of the author's plan. He tells the tale, instead of merely citing the inci-dent, because he cannot assume, as a modern may, that his readers are familiar with it.

In the second place, the critics are confused by a class of mediæval works published (like our books of ana or dictionaries of phrase and fable) for the express purpose of making information accessible. To regard such miscellanies as characteristic of the mediæval mind, or to apply to them the canons of methodical criticism, is absurd. One might as well find fault with a cyclopædia for changing the subject so often, or berate Southey's Commonplace Book for its violation of the dramatic unities.

Finally, there are certain mediæval works of great distinction in which a tale or an allegory is utilized by the author as a vehicle for his own ideas on many subjects. Here the ostensible plan or programme is of no moment or significance. What we have is a series of essays, long and short. Each should be judged by itself, as we judge the essays of Montaigne or Bacon. A famous instance is Jean de Meun, in his continuation of the Romance of the Rose. Jean is quite as interesting a personality as Montaigne, and he has things to say that are every bit as valuable. We should not be misled because he wrote in verse, and chose to string his observations on a thread of allegory instead of dividing them into books and chapters.

Most, if not all, of the so-called digressions in the Canterbury Tales are made by the teller of the story, not by the author. In other words, they are, in each case, a definite part of the dramatic plan; they grow out of the character or the situation. In the Wife of Bath's Tale, for example, the long curtain lecture which the loathly lady delivers to her disconsolate husband, is in perfect accord with the worthy Wife's own argumentative habits, as described and illustrated in her prologue. Even the parade of learning is in character. The Wife had heard much literature, as we know, from her fifth husband, the clerk of Oxford, who was never tired of reading aloud to her, particularly from works that slandered women.

Sometimes, indeed, the inserted occasional matter is more valuable than the story itself. In the Sumner's Tale, a sordid comic anecdote is made the occasion for a vivid and deliciously humorous account of the methods of a begging friar. In the Merchant's Tale, a cynical fabliau is expanded by discussion and comment into a savage satire on husbands and wives, from the point of view (be it always remembered) not of Geoffrey Chaucer, but of the disillusioned Merchant, who has been married but two months and is seeking solace in a pilgrimage to St. Thomas. In the Nun's Priest's Tale, a simple fable grows, by characteristic insertions and development, into a masterpiece of the mock heroic.

It has long been the fashion to divide Chaucer's poetical activity into three periods, — the French, the Italian, and the English. This plan has a neat and almost epigrammatic symmetry which commends it to orderly minds, and it is undeniably convenient. The trouble is, that the three adjectives — *French, Italian,* and *English* — do not apply to their several periods with anything like the same degree of descriptive accuracy.

In the French Period, Chaucer was literally under the control of French methods and French conventions, — a disciple of Guillaume de Lorris and Guillaume de Machaut. He was, to all intents and purposes, a French love-poet writing (so it happened) in the English language.

In the Italian period, on the contrary, Chaucer was nobody's disciple. Dante and Petrarch and Boccaccio did not control him: they were his emancipators. They enlarged his horizon. They awoke him to consciousness of power that was his own. Boccaccio, in particular, did him the priceless service of stirring him to emulation. Here, in the Teseide and the Filostrato, were new and fine and congenial things: not unapproachable masterpieces, like the ancient classics, but works that he might hope to equal, that he might even aspire to surpass. He had learned much from the Frenchmen, and all that was of value in what they taught him, he of course retained. This second period, then, is not Italian in the sense in which the first is French. It was a time of originality. Chaucer had risen to the height of his powers, though their full sweep, their scope and compass, might be still in the future.

And finally, the third period is called "English" (with still another shift in the application) not because Chaucer was ruled by English fashions (as by French fashions in the French period) nor yet because he was inspired and emancipated by English writers (as by Italians in the Italian period), but because his genius turned to English life and English character.

Thus our three adjectives — pat as they seem — are not at actual parity. Chaucer's French period is French in a sense in which his Italian period is not Italian, and his English period is English in still a different signification.

Besides, this neat triplicity obscures the whole process of Chaucer's career, which, of course, was cumulative. Chaucer did not forget French when he studied Italian, and he took with him into the English period all the lessons he had ever learned.

There is one more objection to the sacred number three: — it ought to be four. Between the French and the Italian Period we must admit a Period of Transition.

Chaucer first visited Italy in 1373. His journey (including the time spent in travel) occupied exactly 174 days. Three or four months will cover his residence in Italy, and, while there, he was neither stationary nor at leisure: he went to Genoa and Florence, and in both places was busy with the king's affairs. Doubtless he brought home some manuscripts; but it was not, in all probability, until he reached London that he gave them any studious attention. The Italian Period, in all conscience, should not begin until he undertook the Palamon or the Troilus, whichever came first: that is, not, I suppose, until about 1380 or 1382. Meanwhile, after 1373, Chaucer was assimilating Italian poetry, was winning, under its guidance, more and more emancipation from French fashions, and was training himself for the full scope and exercise of his native power. Within the Period of Transition, likewise, came an enormous extension of Chaucer's general reading, particularly in Latin. With Ovid he had long been familiar. But it was in this period, apparently, — and certainly in the decade following the writing of the Book of the Duchess in 1369 — that he read Virgil and

Lucan and Statius. Here, too, must fall his reading of the Consolation of Philosophy. Besides, he
broadened his knowledge of history and of the
great cycles of romance. The vision of Fame's
Palace affords us a truly remarkable list of names
of authors, with many of whom Chaucer had become familiar. How he did it, we learn from the
poem itself, — by shutting himself up in his
chamber, after his day's work at the custom
house, and sitting ever "at another book" until
his eyes were dazed and dull.

Next to Shakspere, Chaucer is the greatest
delineator of character in our literature.

Mediæval characterization was almost purely
typical. Chaucer vitalized the types. This great
feat he accomplished, first by his humorous and
pathetic realism, and, secondly, by his dramatic
power, — by which I mean, of course, his ability
to put himself into the place of various men and
women, and then to express their nature in
speech and action.

There is a vast difference — it is abysmal, even
— between reverting to the middle ages, and
living in them. It is no less than the difference
between romance and reality. Those critics, and
their name is legion, who cannot or will not see
this difference, had better shut their books,
which they have not the skill to read, and mingle
for a day or two with their fellow-creatures.

They might not cease from troubling, even then,
but they would give the weary, rest.

Chaucer lived a full life in a world of contemporary men and women, which he knew and
loved. It was not a fool's paradise, nor yet a
Land of Cockayne, but a hard, practical, bus-
tling, struggling, delightful age — *le siècle où nous
vivons*. And it had its conventional rules, in art,
in literature, in science, in religion (even as you
and I!), and five of them, I dare say, were wise,
and five were foolish. And Chaucer submitted
himself to the rules, and played the game as they
directed, and was all the better for it. Incidentally, he was endowed at birth with the splendid
accident of genius, but it did not poison his cup.
He saw the irony of circumstance, or fate, or
what you will, pervading human life, as no artic-
ulate-speaking man has ever seen it before or
since. But he did not mistake himself for the
centre of the system. It was tragedy, no doubt,
that Cressida, at the very moment of her treason
to Troilus, should swear, in her heart, to keep
faith with her new lover: —

"To Diomede algate I wol be trewe!"

But it was comedy that Geoffrey Chaucer, prince
of poets, should make his living by "controlling"
the king's customs and repairing the dykes at
Greenwich. This divine gift of humor preserved

him from the abject vice of self-pity. He had too
sound a nature to "thank whatever gods there
were for his indomitable soul."

Almost all Chaucer's references to himself are
ironical. He is an outsider — so he tells us —
in the courts of love, the *servus servorum* of the
god. He invents nothing: all his work is that of
a faithful copyist. In the Troilus he follows Lol-
lius humbly, neither adding nor subtracting: he
cannot help it, for he has no "sentiment" — no
feeling or perception in these matters; and therefore he asks no thanks, and hopes to escape censure for whatever faults the reader may discover.
In the Canterbury Tales, he is scrupulous to
report the stories word for word, exactly as the
Pilgrims told them, whether their style or substance was courtly or "churlish." His wit is
thin. He cannot even marshal his travelling
companions in the order of their rank in society.
He has no skill in versification, and his English
is too crude to do justice to elevated themes.
When his turn comes, he can only rehearse an
ancient doggerel rhyme — a deal of skimble-
skamble stuff which makes poor Harry Bailly's
ears ache. And when he is interrupted, he has
no more poetry to offer, but spins instead a long
prose allegory, which only a sturdy specialist can
read.

Can we see *the man*, then? Yes, in all essentials, for the irony helps, not hinders, and there is evidence in plenty.

Chaucer had an immense enthusiasm for life in this world; for the society of his fellow-creatures, high and low, good and bad; for real men and women — knights and sumners, millers and parsons, monks and merchants, delicate cloistered ladies and boisterous wives of Bath. Whatever was good of its kind was a delight to him. And he had such stupendous luck in always meeting nonpareils! There was no better priest than the Parson anywhere; no such Pardoner from one end of England to the other; never so great a purchaser as the Man of Law. If you sought from Hull to Carthage, you couldn't find a mariner to match the Shipman. The Wife of Bath was so excellent a cloth-maker that she actually beat the Dutch. The Sumner's bass voice was more than twice as loud as a trumpet. The Friar was the best beggar in his convent. Why, when the rascally alchemist came riding post-haste to join the Pilgrims, whom he hoped to interest in some of his confidence games, he was perspiring so admirably that Chaucer gazed at him with rapture. "It was joye for to seen him swete!" cries the poet in high delight. A joy indeed, — he did it in such a thoroughly competent way!

Let us not make the common mistake of thinking that Chaucer liked his scallawags better than the respectable members of the company, or the still grosser error of supposing that he satirized the Church. He shows every bit as much power and personal interest in describing the good parson as in describing the worldly monk or the merry friar. Chaucer took his religion seriously, and gives no hint of unsteadiness in his theological views. He was neither an ascetic nor a devotee: he was a man of the world, "of little abstinence." But he certainly regarded himself as a Christian, and I suspect he knew, for I have a high opinion of his intelligence.

Of personal epistles, to friends or patrons, Chaucer must have written many in the graceful and fashionable form of the balade. We can but lament the loss of these pieces, which, apart from their literary value, would be priceless for the light they would throw upon Chaucer the man. Only a few of them have come down to us.

One of these, the Balade of Good Counsel, has recently been recognized, by a clever American woman, as an address to Sir Philip la Vache, a man of mark in his day; it is charming, but tells us nothing about the author. The Complaint to his Empty Purse deplores a condition too common with poets, and others, to be especially significant, except of the easy terms on which Chaucer stood with King Henry IV. The Envoy

to Bukton has been maltreated by biographers.
It is immensely interesting for its mention of
the Wife of Bath, with a plain allusion to her
heretical tenet about the sovereignty of wives
over their husbands. This great comic character,
we are permitted to infer, had become almost
proverbial among Chaucer's friends and readers.
As to marriage, which is the ostensible subject
of the Envoy, the poem is no more significant of
Chaucer's views or experiences than a comic
valentine now-a-days with regard to its sender's
feelings on the subject of love. Bukton was soon
to take a wife, and Chaucer sent him a jocose
copy of verses, warning him of the traditional
woes of wedlock. The thing may well have been
read at a farewell dinner, amidst the inextinguishable laughter of the blessed bachelors.

The best of them all is the charming Envoy to
Scogan. Chaucer was at Greenwich, — a place
inhabited, according to Harry Bailly, by many a
rascal, — engaged in the responsible but unpoet-
ical task of overseeing the repairs on the dykes
and ditches which confined the Thames and
drained the vast marshes in the neighborhood. A
flood of rain had impeded his work and made his
situation pretty irksome. Scogan was a young
gentleman in high favor at court, and a humble
disciple of Chaucer in poetry. By a humorous
application of astrology to the principles of chiv-

alric love, Chaucer makes Scogan personally responsible for the rainy weather. Venus is weeping, he avers, because Scogan is a renegade: he has sworn to renounce allegiance to his lady at Michaelmas, on account of her hardness of heart. Then there is a sudden turn, which gives to this clever bit of persiflage the value of a *cri du cœur*. "You will say, my friend, that all this is only old Chaucer's fashion of joking in rhyme. Far from it, my dear fellow! I am in no mood for versing. My Muse is rusty, and it is long since I have taken her out of my pencase. Never mind, — this is a transitory world —

> But al shal passe, that men prose or ryme;
> Take every man hys turn, as for his tyme.

We poets come and go, and so do the writers of prose, who take themselves so seriously. All that we can expect is to have our turn, and mine, I think, has gone by. Who can write poetry in Greenwich, in the midst of the rascals and the rain?" Then comes another change of mood, for the poem is like an April day in England, or New England either, for that matter. "Good-bye, Scogan. Remember me at court! Perhaps a word dropped in the proper quarter may give me a better berth. But, whatever you do, see that you never renounce love again, now that you know how your misconduct affects the weather."

I have spent so much time on this trifle, thrown off by the poet in a moment of comic exasperation, because I believe it to be the only bit of real autobiography, except the lines to Adam Scrivener and a short passage in the House of Fame, that we have from Chaucer's pen. What would you give, O critic, to have been the rain-soaked Greenwich rascal who carried Chaucer's official report to Windsor, and along with it this little letter, meant only for Master Henry Scogan's private eye?

II

THE BOOK OF THE DUCHESS

FOUR dreadful plagues laid England waste in Chaucer's lifetime. In the third of these, in 1369, died Queen Philippa and her daughter-in-law Blanche, the wife of John of Gaunt, Duke of Lancaster. Chaucer and his wife, also named Philippa, were both attached to the royal household, and they received an allowance of black cloth for mourning.

So far as we know, Chaucer paid no tribute of verse to the memory of the good queen, whom all men loved. Probably none was expected. King Edward had but slight acquaintance with the English language, and no interest at all in English literature. His son John, however, belonged to Chaucer's generation, — they were of almost exactly the same age, — and he doubtless requested the poet to write an elegy: we should rather say "commanded," since we are speaking of a prince of the blood. That the commission was grateful to Chaucer's feelings we may well believe; for the Book of the Duchess is instinct with sadness. True, Chaucer does not lament this great lady in his own person, but that is due to his exquisite and admirable art. He detaches himself completely, to concentrate our attention on the theme, which is, as it ought to be, the bitter grief of the despairing husband, who has lost the love of his youth, and can think of nothing but her gracious perfections.

This artistic detachment, which becomes from this time forward a marked feature of Chaucer's method, is achieved in the present instance by a skilful use of familiar conventions. The elegy is cast into the form of a vision. The poet tells the story of a dream: how, wandering in a wood, he fell in with a stranger knight in black garments, and asked and received an explanation of his sorrow. The poet expresses the deepest sympathy. Though himself in trouble, as we learn from the prologue, he ignores his own woes utterly in his effort to console the stranger, and does not remember them when he wakes, so profound is the impression of the haunting dream.

> Thoghte I, "Thys ys so queynt a sweven
> That I wol, be processe of tyme,
> Fonde to put this sweven in ryme
> As I kan best, and that anoon."
> This was my sweven; now hit ys doon.

Thus, by a delicate and well-imagined fiction, the artist Chaucer can hold his attitude of detachment, so vital to the effect of the composition, while, at the same time, Chaucer the

humble friend can suggest, without obtrusive-
ness, his respectful and affectionate sympathy
with the ducal house.

The substance of the elegy, by this adjust-
ment, is spoken, not written merely; and it is
spoken by the lady's husband, who can best
describe her beauty, her charm of manner, and
all her gracious qualities of mind and heart.
Thus we have in the Book of the Duchess, not a
prostrate and anxiously rhetorical obituary, from
the blazoning pen of a commissioned laureate,
but a tribute of pure love from the lady's equal,
who can speak without constraint, — from her
husband, who has most cause to mourn as he has
best knowledge of what he has lost.

Let us follow the course of the story in brief,
preserving, if we can, that simplicity of language
which is one of its distinguishing traits. The
Dreamer is speaking, and he begins his prologue
with an ejaculation of artless astonishment: —

I have great wonder that I am still alive, for I have
had no sleep this long time. Hopeless love gives me no
rest. It amazes me that a man can live so long, and suffer so much, and sleep so little. I should think he would
die. One night, a little while ago, weary from lack of
sleep, I bade my servant bring me a book to pass the
time away, and I began to read it, sitting up in my bed.
It was a volume of old stories, and one of them was
Ovid's tale of Ceyx and Alcyone. It told how King
Ceyx was lost at sea, and how Queen Alcyone, in anxiety
and distress, prayed Juno to vouchsafe her a dream,

that she might know whether her husband was alive or dead. And Juno despatched her messenger to the God of Sleep, and he, obeying her command, sent the drowned Ceyx to Alcyone in a vision. He stood at the foot of her bed, and called her by name, and told her of his fate, and bade her bury his body, which she should find cast up on the shore: —

> "And farewel, swete, my worldes blysse!
> I praye God youre sorwe lysse.
> To lytel while oure blysse lasteth!"

Alcyone awoke, and mourned, and died ere the third morrow.

I was astonished at this tale, for I had never heard of any gods that could send sleep to weary men; and straightway I made a vow to Morpheus, or Juno, or whatever divinity it might be that had such power. Scarcely had I finished speaking when I fell fast asleep over my book, and I had a wonderful dream, which I do not believe even Joseph or Macrobius could interpret. I will tell you what it was.

So ends the prologue, which not only serves as a felicitous introduction to the vision that is to follow, but gives us, in perfection, the atmosphere, the mood, of the piece, — love and sorrow and bereavement. It shows us, too, the Dreamer in complete psychic sympathy with the subject; for what could be more natural than that he should dream of some bereavement or other, when his mind was full of the piteous tale of Alcyone, and the background of his thought was his own suffering for hopeless love?

I dreamt that it was May, and that I was awaked by the singing of the birds upon my chamber roof. My windows were of stained glass, figuring the tale of Troy, and the walls were painted with the whole story of the Romance of the Rose. The sun streamed in upon my bed, for there was not a cloud in the sky. And as I lay, I heard a huntsman blow his horn, and the noise of men and horses and hounds; and I arose, and took my horse, and rode out into the field, and joined the hunters, who were hastening toward the forest. Then I asked a fellow who was leading a hound in a leash, "Who is hunting here?" "Sir," said he, "the emperor Octavian, and he is close by." So the hunt began. The hart was found, and the dogs were uncoupled. But soon he stole away, and the huntsman blew a "forloyn" at the last.

I left the tree where I had been posted; and a little puppy, that had followed the hounds, but was too young to keep up with them, came and fawned upon me, and crept up humbly, with joined ears, as if he had known me; but when I would have caught him, he ran away. I followed down a grassy path, with flowers underfoot, that led through the wood, till at last I was aware of a young knight in black clothes, who sat under a tree, and he was composing a bitter complaint — a kind of song — of the death of his lady. I greeted him courteously, but he neither heard nor saw me, so full of sorrow was he. By-and-by he looked up, and I asked his forgiveness for disturbing him. But he took no offence, and was very gracious, despite his sorrow, and seemed willing to talk with me. So I begged him to tell me his grief, saying that I would help him if I could, and that even to speak of it might ease his heart.

Then he burst out into a piteous lament. Nothing, he said, would do him any good. His laughter had turned to weeping, his glad thoughts to heaviness, his day to night, his valor to shame. For he had played at chess with Fortune, and she had taken his queen, and checkmated him. But he could not blame her: he would have done as much, had he been Fortune; for, said he, "I dare well say she took the best! But by that game of chess, I have lost all my happiness, and there is nothing left for me but death."

Now, when I heard this story, I could scarce stay there longer, for pity. I besought him not to kill himself, for then he would lose his soul. And I told him that no man alive would make all this woe, just for losing a queen at chess. "Why!" cried the knight, "you do not understand me! I have lost more than you imagine."

So I begged him to leave his riddles, and tell me plainly what had plunged him into such distress. And he assented, if I would promise to hear him to the end. I swore to listen, and to understand, so far as I had wit. Then he told me the story of his life. How from his earilest youth he had served the god of love. Yet it was many a year before he set his heart on any lady. He had always longed for the time to come, and prayed ever to the god to vouchsafe that he might fall in love with one that should be beautiful and gracious. And once upon a time, so he said, he came into a place where there was the fairest company of ladies ever seen. But one surpassed them all, as the summer's sun outshines the moon or the seven stars. And he took no counsel but of her eyes and his own heart, for it seemed to him that it would be far better to serve her in vain than to win the love of any other woman in the world.

Then he told me of her beauty, and all her charming ways. There was no dulness where she was: she was neither too quiet nor too merry; and her speech — how goodly it was, and how soft! She was never scornful; no man or woman was wounded by her tongue, and her word was as true as any bond, and she knew not how to chide. Then the knight told me the lady's name. It was "good, fair White" [that is, Blanche], and well did it accord with her loveliness.

"Truly," said I, when the knight paused a moment, "your love was well bestowed. I know not how you could have done better." "Better?" cried he. "Nay, no wight so well!" "So I suppose," was my reply, "I am sure you believe what you say." [For of course, the Dreamer, as a loyal lover, must not admit that any lady can surpass his own *amie*.] "Why!" cried the knight, "all that saw her said, and swore, that she was the best and fairest. She was as good as Penelope of Greece or the noble wife Lucretia. When I first saw her, I was young, and scarce knew what love meant; yet I gave all my childish mind to the emprise. And still she sits in my heart and verily I would not let her pass out of my thought for all this world."

Then I asked the knight to tell me how he first spoke with the lady, and how she knew that he loved her, and then to vouchsafe to explain what the loss was that he had mentioned before. "Nay!" cried the knight again, "you know not what you say. I have lost more than you imagine." "How so?" I asked. "What is your loss? Does she refuse to love you? Or have you done aught amiss, so that she has forsaken you? For God's sake, tell me the whole story!"

Then he told me how he first declared his love. Long it was before he dared, and then he stammered, and forgot his fine speeches, and hung his head for shame, and could utter only one word "Mercy!" and no more. At last his courage came again, and he besought her to accept his humble service; but it was yet a long time before she returned his love. Then his joy was perfect. He was as one raised from death to life. "Thus we lived," said the knight, "for many a year in perfect harmony. Our hearts were so even a pair that neither suffered nor rejoiced without the other."

Once more I asked the knight a question: "Sir," said I, "where is she now?" "Now?" said he. "Alas that I was born! That was the loss that I told you of. Remem-

ber how I said, 'You know not what you mean. I have
lost more than you imagine!' God knows, alas! that
was she!"

> Therwith he wax as ded as stoon,
> And seyde, "Allas, that I was bore!
> That was the los that here-before
> I tolde the that I hadde lorn.
> Bethenke how I seyde here-beforn,
> 'Thow wost ful lytel what thow menest;
> I have lost more than thow wenest' —
> God wot, allas! ryght that was she!"
> "Allas, sir, how? what may that be?"
> "She ys ded!" "Nay!" "Yis, be my trouthe!"
> "Is that youre los? Be God, hyt ys routhe!"
> And with that word ryght anoon
> They gan to strake forth; al was doon,
> For that tyme, the hert-huntyng.
> With that me thoghte that this kyng
> Gan homwardes for to ryde
> Unto a place, was there besyde,
> Which was from us but a lyte.
> A long castel with walles white,
> Be seynt Johan! on a ryche hil
> As me mette; but thus hyt fil.
> Ryght thus me mette, as I yow telle,
> That in the castell ther was a belle,
> As hyt hadde smyten houres twelve. —
> Therwyth I awook myselve
> And fond me lyinge in my bed;
> And the book that I hadde red,
> Of Alcione and Seys the kyng,
> And of the goddes of slepyng,
> I fond hyt in myn hond ful even.
> Thoghte I, "Thys ys so queynt a sweven
> That I wol, be processe of tyme,
> Fonde to put this sweven in ryme

As I kan best, and that anoon."
This was my sweven; now hit ys doon.

The first thing that strikes one in reading the
Book of the Duchess is the quality of artlessness
or *naïveté*, to which, indeed, the poem owes much
of its charm. This challenges instant attention,
for naïveté is often rated as one of Chaucer's
permanent traits. As such, it holds a conspicuous place in ten Brink's classic inventory of his
literary characteristics, along with "fondness for
the description of psychological states or conditions," "effective pathos," and "a tendency to
humorous realism."

Now few facts of history, be it sacred or profane, are more solidly established than that
Geoffrey Chaucer, in his habit as he lived, was
not naïf. Whatever one may think of our American practice in the appointment of diplomatists,
it is quite certain that, in the fourteenth century,
men were not selected by the English king to
negotiate secret affairs on the Continent because
they were innocent and artless. And even so, a
naïf Collector of Customs would be a paradoxical
monster.

Besides, whatever else he may have been,
Chaucer was admittedly a humorist, and naïveté
is incompatible with a sense of humor. If I am
artless, I may make you laugh; but the sense of
humor, in that case, is yours, not mine. The

source of your amusement, in fact, will be your keen perception of the incongruity between my childlike seriousness and the absurdity of what I have said or done. Hence, if I myself am a humorist, I may assume naïveté, from my own perception of the incongruous, in order to lend my words additional effect. This, of course, is the principle which underlies the rule that a jester must look as grave as he can; or, to put the precept in its crudely familiar guise, "Don't laugh at your own jokes!"

Real naïveté, as everybody knows, gives a person an appearance of innocence and helplessness, and will therefore be amusing, or pathetic, or both at once, according to the subject or the situation. As a trick of art, therefore, we expect to find the ingenuous manner adopted, now for purposes of humor, and now for those of pathos.

I should apologize abjectly for parading these truisms, were it not that they have been so continually overlooked in the literary criticism of Chaucer as to lead to frequent confusion between the artist and the man. And this confusion is exhibited at its very worst in the ordinary appraisal of the Book of the Duchess.

In this elegy, the device, I need not say, is employed to heighten the pathos. It deserves our earnest attention. For we shall immediately discover that certain supposed flaws — not in the main design, which is unassailable, but in this or that detail — are due to Chaucer's use of this artistic expedient, and not to feebleness of grasp or a wavering vision.

In the first place, the effect of artlessness in the poem is produced by extreme simplicity in style and versification. That the simplicity results from lack of skill is, I fancy, a proposition that nobody will maintain, though it has often been taken for granted (may I say *naïvely?*) by critics who ought to know better. Consider the following passage, where Chaucer is describing, with the swift and terse precision of his best narrative art, the apparition of Alcyone's drowned husband: —

> Anoon this god of slep abrayd
> Out of hys slep, and gan to goon,
> And dyde as he had bede hym doon;
> Took up the dreynte body sone
> And bar hyt forth to Alcione,
> Hys wif the quene, ther as she lay
> Ryght even a quarter before day,
> And stood ryght at hyr beddes fet,
> And called hir ryght as she het
> By name, and sayde, "My swete wyf,
> Awake! let be your sorwful lyf!
> For in your sorwe there lyth no red.
> For, certes, swete, I nam but ded;
> Ye shul me never on lyve yse.
> But, goode swete herte, that ye
> Bury my body, for such a tyde
> Ye mowe hyt fynde the see besyde;

And farewel, swete, my worldes blysse!
I praye God youre sorwe lysse.
To lytel while oure blysse lasteth!"

Whoever hugs the delusion that because the diction and the metre are simple, it is easy to write like this, is humbly besought to try his hand at imitating The Vicar of Wakefield, or Andrew Marvell's Song of the Emigrants in Bermuda.

Let us pass to a consideration a little more debatable, but equally certain in the upshot.

There are two characters in the Book of the Duchess — the Dreamer, who tells the story, and the Knight in Black. Now the Knight is not naïf at all. On the contrary, he is an adept in the courtly conventions, which have become a part of his manner of thought and speech. He is a finished gentleman of a period quite as studied as the Elizabethan in its fashions of conduct and discourse. All the naïveté is due to the Dreamer, whose character is sharply contrasted with that of the Knight. The Dreamer speaks in the first person. One might infer, therefore, that he is Geoffrey Chaucer, but that would be an error: he is a purely imaginary figure, to whom certain purely imaginary things happen, in a purely imaginary dream. He is as much a part of the fiction in the Book of the Duchess as the Merchant or the Pardoner or the Host is a part of the fiction in the Canterbury Tales.

The mental attitude of the Dreamer is that of childlike wonder. He understands nothing, not even the meaning of his dream. He can only tell what happened, and leave the interpretation to us. Let us revert to our summary: "I have great wonder that I am still alive; for I cannot sleep for sorrow and I am ever in fear of death. One night, not long ago, I was reading an old book, and I found a story in it about the God of Sleep. It astonished me, for I had never heard of him before. And so I vowed to give him a feather bed if he would send me slumber. And straightway I fell asleep over my book; and I had a dream which makes me wonder whenever I think of it. I will tell you what it was."

When we come to the Knight in Black and his pathetic history, the Dreamer is true to his nature of gentle simplicity — always wondering and never understanding. He wonders what makes the knight so sad; and when the knight tries to tell him, he still wonders, and still questions. Hints and half-truths and figures of speech are lost upon him, until at last the knight, in despair, as it seems, at his questioner's lack of comprehension, comes out plainly with the bare fact: "She is dead." "No!" says the Dreamer, still with his air of innocent surprise. "Yea, sir," replies the knight, "that is what I have all this time been trying to tell you. That is the 'loss' I mentioned long ago." Even then the Dreamer has little to say. He can only speak the language of nature and simplicity: "Is that your loss? By God, it is a pity!" And then he dreamt that the hunt was over, and a clock in a tower struck twelve, and he awoke, and there he was — lying in bed, with his book of ancient stories still in his hand. And so he wonders more than ever. He does not know what the dream means, or whether it means anything at all. But it was a strange dream, truly, and full of charm, and he decides to write it out as well as he can, before he forgets it.

This childlike Dreamer, who never reasons, but only feels and gets impressions, who never knows what anything means until he is told in the plainest language, is not Geoffrey Chaucer, the humorist and man of the world. He is a creature of the imagination, and his childlikeness is part of his dramatic character.

For almost half a century, by record, the literal-minded have rehearsed, over and over again, their obvious censure on the construction of this beautiful elegy. Chaucer, they allege, is ridiculously obtuse. He hears the knight composing a dirge on his dead lady, and sees that he is dressed in mourning; yet he keeps asking him "what he has lost," and is thunderstruck at the final revelation. Substitute for "Chaucer," in these strictures, "the Dreamer," and they are half-answered already. For the Dreamer is not merely artless by nature; he is dulled, and almost stupefied, by long suffering. So he tells us at the very first: — "I am, as it were, a man in a maze. I take heed of nothing, how it comes or goes. Naught is to me either pleasant or unpleasant. I have no feeling left, whether for good or bad."

This is not all. The Knight in Black, unaware that the Dreamer has overheard the dirge, takes pains to mystify him at the outset with an allegory of Fortune and the chess-play, and evades his subsequent questions as long as evasion is possible. For the knight, though eager to talk, shrinks from uttering the bare and brutal truth: — "She is dead!" Speech eases his soul. It is a tender joy to describe his lady's beauty, to dilate on his own childish years and his innocent worship of love, to tell of their first meeting among a goodly company, to remember how abashed he was when he tried to reveal his devotion. It is a relief to him that the Dreamer seems not to comprehend.

But what of the Dreamer? Is he really deaf and blind to what he hears and sees? By no means! Artless he is, and unsuspicious, and dull with sorrow and lack of sleep; but the dirge is too clear for even him to misunderstand. "My lady is dead," so ran the words, "and gone away from

me. Alas, death! why did you not take me likewise when you took her?" The Dreamer knows
perfectly well that the lady is dead. What then?
Does Chaucer straightway make him forget?
The blunder would be incredible. Chaucer may
have been an immature artist when he devised
this situation, but he was not a fool; and if, in the
haste of writing, he had momentarily entangled
himself in such a confusion, all he had to do was
to strike out the dirge. The excision of thirteen
lines, without the change of a word beside, would
have removed the stumbling block — and there
are more than thirteen hundred verses in the
elegy!

In fact, however, there is no confusion. The
Dreamer knows that the lady is dead, but he
wishes to learn more, not from idle curiosity, but
out of sympathetic eagerness to afford the knight
the only help in his power — the comfort of pour-
ing his sad story into compassionate ears. And
he tells us as much, in the plainest language.

> Anoon ryght I gan fynde a tale
> To hym, to loke wher I myght ought
> Have more knowynge of hys thought.[1]

He owes his knowledge of the lady's death to
overhearing the knight, who was too much ab-
sorbed to notice either his steps or his greeting.
With instinctive delicacy, therefore, he sup-

[1] Verses 536–538.

presses this knowledge, and invites the knight's confidence in noncommittal terms, on the ground of pity for his obvious suffering. And when the knight speaks eagerly, though not plainly, as we have seen, and the Dreamer notes that words are indeed a relief, as he had hoped, it is not for him to check their flow. Let him rather hide his knowledge still, and tempt the knight to talk on and on. It is the artless artfulness of a kindly and simple nature.

Thus, by the interplay of two contrasted characters, — the naïf and sympathizing Dreamer and the mourning knight, who is not naïf at all, — brought together in a situation in which the Dreamer, impelled by simple kindliness, conceals his knowledge in order to tempt the knight to relieve his mind by talking, Chaucer has effected a climax of emotional suspense which culminates in the final disclosure. The conclusion is beyond all praise. "Where is she now?" the Dreamer asks. "Oh!" says the knight, coming out at last with the hideous fact that he could not bring himself to utter before, "she is dead." "Is that your loss? By God, it is ruth!" And with that the hunt was over, and a bell struck twelve in the dream castle, — was it a real sound this time? — and he awoke and found his book of Ceyx and Alcyone still in his hand.

This outburst is pure nature: it shows us the

Chaucer that is to be when he shall break loose
from contemporary French fashions of allegory
and symbolism and pretty visions and dare to
speak the language of the heart. What can one
say in such a case but "Good God, man, I am
sorry for you!" The rest is silence.

The Book of the Duchess belongs to Chaucer's
early period, when his technique was almost
purely that of the French love-allegory. For his
leading conventions, and for a quantity of details, he is indebted to the Romance of the Rose,
which he had already translated, and to his dis-
tinguished contemporary Guillaume de Machaut.
In his use of this material, however, Chaucer
shows a high degree of originality, both in applying the dream convention to his specific purpose,
and in the imaginative control which he exercises
over the traditional phenomena.

Here, for the first time, whether in French or
English, we find the standard French conventions — the love-vision, and the lover's lament
— turned to the uses of a personal elegy. To dis-
cern their fitness for this particular purpose was
a considerable achievement; for they are, in fact,
quite as well adapted to that end as the pastoral
device, with which we moderns are more familiar,
and which, as in the Lycidas, we accept without
a scruple.

Let us first consider the Prologue, which in-

troduces us to the Dreamer and contains the
Ovidian story of Ceyx and Alcyone.

The situation comes from Le Paradys d'Amours,
a pretty poem by Chaucer's contemporary, Froissart the chronicler, who was no doubt his personal friend. Here, as in the Duchess, the
Dreamer is a woful lover, whose melancholy
will not let him sleep. Froissart also gave Chaucer a suggestion for the mood of gentle sorrow, as
well as for what is so essentially bound up with
that mood — the Dreamer's artlessness. In the
Paradys, however, this trait is not dramatic: it
is merely the reflection of the poet's own nature.
Froissart was, in deed and truth, the most naïf
of men. Intensely susceptible to impressions
from without, he reacted with all the grace of
infancy and all its innocent and subtle charm.
This Chaucer felt when he read the Frenchman's
poem. His artistic instinct recognized its appropriateness to his own elegiac subject; and his
dramatic power enabled him to comprehend and
express. And so he created his Dreamer, and
entrusted the story to him to tell.

I have just said that Froissart gave Chaucer a
suggestion, also, for the mood of his elegy; but
here again it was only a suggestion. For the
Frenchman does not sustain the mood, which to
him was merely an introductory convention.
The Paradys is in no wise elegiac. It begins in a

melancholy strain, but sorrow is not its theme.
It deals with the joy of love, with the comforts
and rewards which the god grants to his faithful
servants. In Chaucer, on the contrary, the
whole poem is developed out of the Dreamer's
mood, which is constant, habitual, and not to be
separated from his character.

In Froissart, then, the situation and the mood
are alike momentary, external, evanescent, —
the only constant element is the writer's own
naïveté. In Chaucer, both the situation and the
mood are involved in the Dreamer's temperament, which, compulsive in its gentle innocence,
unifies the conception, and subdues the whole to
a tone of tender and wistful monody.

Chaucer's indebtedness to Guillaume de
Machaut has long been recognized, but few critics seem to appreciate his skill in adapting the
borrowed material to his main design. Machaut,
in the Fontaine Amoureuse, hears a lover's complaint embodying the legend of Alcyone and
closing with an appeal to Morpheus: — "Let
him take my form, as he took that of Ceyx, and
visit my lady as she sleeps, and tell her how I
suffer. Then I am sure she will relent. I will reward him with a nightcap of peacock's feathers,
that he may sleep the sounder, and a soft bed
stuffed with the plumes of gyrfalcons." The
singer is not speaking for himself. He had com-

posed the lament for a great lord, into whose presence Machaut is straightway conducted. This lord, who is reclining by the border of a crystal fountain, takes the poet into his confidence. Then they both go to sleep, and have a vision of Venus. She promises the young lord her help, and evokes the figure of his lady, who comforts him with a smile and gracious words, and leaves him full of hope.

This is a pretty fancy, and the use of Alcyone's story in the lament is undeniably ingenious. We may even discover a psychological link of cause and effect between its presence there and the vision vouchsafed to the lover. But the psychology is feeble and the connection somewhat remote.

Froissart, at all events, saw no such link, for when he imitated the Fontaine Amoureuse, as he did in his Paradys d'Amours, he omitted the story of Alcyone altogether. He retained the vow to Morpheus, however, substituting a ring for the nightcap and the feather bed, — which, in his innocence, he thought undignified, — and in one respect he made a felicitous alteration: his dreamer *prays only for sleep*, which falls upon him suddenly. But Froissart employs the dream that slumber brings only to transport himself into the conventional garden, where he encounters certain personified abstractions, and is reassured by the god of love, who grants him an audience, and where he finally meets his lady, with whom he has an eminently satisfactory conversation.

Chaucer's procedure, with these two poems in his mind, is in the highest degree illuminating. Like Froissart, he makes his Dreamer pray to Morpheus, but his sense of humor prompts him to discard the ring in favor of the feather bed. Machaut's story of Alcyone he keeps, recurring to Ovid for some details, but he brings it into vital connection not only with the Dreamer's character, but with the substance of the dream as well. The Dreamer sees the bereaved husband because he has just been reading of a similar bereavement. The lack of precise conformity between the impression made upon his waking mind and the image that recurs in slumber is true to dream-psychology. We do not look for absolute identity in such cases. Here Chaucer, unlike his predecessors, shows himself in immediate contact with the facts and experiences of human life — even with the life of dreams.

Undoubtedly Chaucer meant this carrying over of the waking impression into the dream-state to be inferred by his readers, though the naïveté of the Dreamer suppressed all mention of the inference. The fact of such transmission was commonly recognized, and Chaucer has

adverted to it more than once. In the Squire's
Tale we are expressly informed that Canace's
interest in the wonderful mirror was the direct
cause of her dream: —

> And in hire sleep, right for impressioun
> Of hire mirour, she hadde a visioun — [1]

and there is a very illuminating case in the Parliament of Fowls. The poet has been reading
the Somnium Scipionis, and goes to bed in low
spirits: —

> But fynally, my spirit at the laste,
> For wery of my labour al the day,
> Tok reste, that made me to slepe faste,
> And in my slep I mette, as that I lay,
> How Affrican, ryght in the selve aray
> That Scipion hym say byfore that tyde,
> Was come and stod right at my beddes syde.
>
> The wery huntere, slepynge in his bed,
> To wode ayeyn his mynde goth anon;
> The juge dremeth how his plees been sped;
> The cartere dremeth how his cartes gon;
> The riche, of gold; the knyght fyght with his fon;
> The syke met he drynketh of the tonne;
> The lovere met he hath his lady wonne.
>
> Can I not seyn if that the cause were
> For I hadde red of Affrican byforn,
> That made me to mete that he stod there;
> But thus seyde he, "Thow hast the so wel born
> In lokynge of myn olde bok totorn,
> Of which Macrobye roughte nat a lyte,
> That sumdel of thy labour wolde I quyte."

[1] F. 371–372.

Here the connection between the proem and the story, though formally exact, is imaginatively less close and rather more mechanical than in the Book of the Duchess; but it is still quite satisfactory. As Africanus once took his grandson out of this world, and revealed to him the future dwellings of the righteous and the wicked, so now he conducts Chaucer to a park-gate with two inscriptions, one indicating "the blisful place of hertes hele and dedly woundes cure," the other the realm of Danger and Disdain. They enter the park, which proves to be a lover's paradise with the regular landscape, and the usual conventions follow. Africanus is heard of no more — which is very like a dream. The rest of the Parliament does not here concern us.

Passing from the prologue of the Book of the Duchess to the Dream itself, we find that Chaucer uses his literary models with equal skill, and shows a like felicity in converting the standard forms to his immediate needs. His problem, we remember, was to apply the conventional type of "lover's complaint" to the ends of a personal elegy. Two recent poems by Guillaume de Machaut lay ready at hand, the Judgment of the King of Bohemia and the Remedy for Fortune. Chaucer drew freely from both, as well as from his old favorite, the Romance of the Rose, which he had already translated, apparently entire, and long passages of which he must have known by heart.

The plan of the Judgment of the King of Bohemia shows an obvious similarity to that which Chaucer adopted for the Book of the Duchess. I may be allowed to repeat a very brief summary which I have used on another occasion.

On a fine morning in spring, the poet wanders out into a park where there is many a tree and many a blossom. He sits down by a brook, near a beautiful tower, concealing himself under the trees, to hear the birds sing. A lady approaches, accompanied only by a maid and a little dog. She is met by a knight, who greets her politely, but she passes on, without heeding. The knight overtakes her, and addresses her once more. She apologizes for her inattention, remarking that she was buried in thought. They exchange courtesies, and the knight begs to know the cause of her pensive mood, promising to do his best to comfort her. He himself, he avers, is suffering from bitter grief. The lady consents, on condition that the knight will reveal the origin of his own sorrow. Accordingly, they exchange confidences, in the hearing of the poet, whose presence remains unsuspected.

The lady, it appears, has lost her lover by death. The knight's *amie*, on the contrary, is living, but has forsaken him. They dispute as to which case is the harder. William reveals himself, and at his suggestion the question is submitted to the King of Bohemia, who decides that the knight has the best of the argument.

Such general resemblances, to be sure, are of little significance. When, however, we study the details of the Black Knight's story, the obligations of Chaucer to Guillaume de Machaut come out in a way that is almost startling.

The knight, in response to the Dreamer's questioning, goes back to the memories of his boyhood. As long ago as he could remember, he had honored the god of love as his liege lord and submitted his spotless heart to his control. Love was only a sentiment to him in those days, — an aspiration, a vague dream of something beautiful that might come to pass by-and-by. And so, in devout humility, he had ever besought the god to be propitious, and to entrust his heart, at the appointed hour, to the keeping of some lovely and gracious lady. His prayer was answered. He chanced one day to come into an assembly of the fairest ladies ever seen, and one among them surpassed the rest as the summer sun outshines the moon and the seven stars. He "held no counsel but with her eyes and his own heart," and, thus guided, he thought it was better to serve her in vain than to win the favor of any other woman. Long time he worshipped her in secret, afraid to speak; and when at last he took courage to reveal his adoration, he stammered and forgot everything he had to say. She was hard to win, but at length she had pity upon him, and granted him "the noble gift of her mercy." And thus they lived full many a year, in honorable love and perfect harmony.

This part of the poem embodies the famous description of the Duchess Blanche and of her character, which Lowell admired so much and declared "one of the most beautiful portraits of a woman that were ever drawn."

Now there is nothing new in the Black Knight's story, either in form or substance. The experience he describes is typical, and he speaks throughout in the settled language of the chivalric system. Love was the only life that became the gently nurtured, and they alone were capable of love. Submission to the god was their natural duty; in his grace and favor was their only hope; for no man's heart was in his own control. It was the god of love, not the man's choice, that bestowed it, and none could withstand the god's decree.

It is not strange, therefore, that parallel passages may be found in both the Remedy for Fortune and the Judgment of the King of Bohemia. But the facts go far beyond the mere occurrence of stock phrases. Comparison shows, in the clearest manner, that Chaucer has borrowed from these two poems with absolute freedom. Many lines, both in the knight's story and especially in the portrait, are literally translated, and, when this is not the case, it is often manifest that the language or the sentiments of Machaut suggested the idea, or the particular turn, that

Chaucer has adopted. Still other poems of Machaut are laid under occasional contribution. A close study of the relations here briefly indicated is a remarkable lesson in literary craftsmanship. It is also a good illustration of the fact — well-known but continually forgotten, — that there was no such thing as the crime of plagiarism in the middle ages, for every poet took without hesitation "what he thought he might require," and nobody blamed him.

I have no wish to minimize the indebtedness of Chaucer to his French predecessor. Indeed, there is no temptation to err in that way. For Chaucer uses his borrowings with the power of a master, and nowhere in the poem does his originality appear more strikingly than in the description of the Duchess Blanche, — the very place where his indebtedness is most conspicuous. In Machaut, there is much grace and beauty, but the schematism is complete. The lady utters her lament, and the knight responds. There is no genuine dialogue. In the description, Machaut follows the enumerative method so dear to the middle ages, as if he were, in Hamlet's phrase, "dividing" the lady "inventorially." Hair, forehead, eyebrows, eyes, nose, mouth, cheeks, teeth, chin, and complexion are catalogued in scientific order, with some exquisite touches, but with a total effect of absurd formality. The Elizabethans knew the method well. It was, in truth, inherited from their schematic forefathers, along with many other legacies of thought and style which the sciolists who decry the study of "mediævalism" do vainly misinterpret. Olivia makes merry with such stilted accumulation of details in her "Item, two lips, indifferent red."

But Chaucer knew that one should not "make so long a tale of the straw as of the corn," and, in the very act of borrowing from Machaut, he has avoided this fault, though it is one to which the rapid and garrulous short couplet might well have tempted him beyond resistance. In the Black Knight's description of his lady, we find the same admirable selective art that distinguishes the later work of the poet. Chaucer's knight declares that he cannot describe his lady's face — it passes his ability in expression; but he dwells lovingly on her hair, and lingers over the description of her eyes, which were not too wide open:—

> "Were she never so glad,
> Hyr lokynge was not foly sprad,
> Ne wildely, thogh that she pleyde;
> But ever, me thoght, hir eyen seyde,
> 'Be God, my wrathe ys al foryive!'"

This trait, one is surprised to discover, is taken from Machaut. Yet we cannot doubt that it was true to the life in the case of the Duchess Blanche. Apparently it was the fashion for ladies to let their eyelids droop a little, with what used to be called a languishing look. In *his* lady, the knight protests, this was not an affectation:—

> "Hyt was hir owne pure lokyng
> That the goddesse, dame Nature,
> Had mad hem opene by mesure,
> And close."

This is not in Machaut, where also we miss the exquisite couplet closing with "My wrathe is al foryive!" The whole description is so broken up, in Chaucer, as to produce precisely that effect of artless inevitableness that the occasion requires. The mourning knight is not describing his lady: he is giving voice to his unstudied recollection — now of her nature, now of her beauty, now of her demeanor, now of her speech — spasmodically, in no order, as this or that idea rises in his agitated mind.

That Chaucer should adopt the fiction of a dream, both here and elsewhere, needs no explanation; for it was one of the favorite devices of his age, as of the age preceding and of that which followed. What challenges attention is the frequency with which he adverts to the philosophy of dreams. Not that he has anything new to say. The subject had been exhausted by the philosophers, and he could merely ponder over their theories and observations, at a loss for a solution of problems that still puzzle some of the best heads amongst us. He deals with the topic in the Parliament of Fowls, at the beginning of the House of Fame, with extraordinary vividness in the last book of the Troilus,[1] and with all his wit and humor in the discussion between Chanticleer and Pertelote. Dreams play as large a rôle in Chaucer as presentiments do in Shakspere. We may guess, if we like, that Shakspere was in his own person susceptible to presentiments and that Chaucer, for his part, had uncommonly vivid dreams. If so, this consideration reduces the amount of convention and increases the proportion of fact in Chaucer's employment of the device. All this not by way of apology, where none is needed, but as an observation worth making, whether it is valid or not — a point that is none the less interesting because it can never be decided. The world is well acquainted with inspiration that comes in sleep; and English literary history does not lack its examples, from Cædmon at Whitby to Coleridge and his Kubla Khan.

Chaucer, then, in casting the Book of the Duchess into the form of a dream, was faithful to a prevalent fashion. When, however, we compare his dream-poem with its predecessors, we are at once aware of an essential difference. Their dreams are a mere device to get the reader

[1] v. 245–266, 316–322, 358–385.

into a sort of fairyland, a mediæval Arcadia, peopled by personified abstractions — Hope and Mercy and Desire and Jealousy and Despair — or by typical lovers scarcely more concrete than the abstractions themselves. The dream-machinery is often handled with no little skill, and there is at times an atmosphere of unreality which appealed to our forefathers as a welcome relief from the tumult and ugliness of every day. But there is no attempt to reproduce the actual phenomena of dreams. The author goes to sleep at the beginning of his poem and wakes up at the end. In the interim, he may be in a strange country, perhaps, but he is not in any dreamland that mortals know.

But Chaucer had a strong sense of fact, and his Book of the Duchess is really like a dream. This effect, which every reader must instantly admit, is partly due to the naïveté of the Dreamer's temperament, which we contemplate, as we read, with something of that tolerant superiority with which we remember, in our waking moments, the innocent faith we have accorded to the irrationalities of dreamland. In part, however, this effect of dreaming is produced by a number of delicate touches, almost too elusive to isolate, but undeniably significant in their total impression.

The first of these touches, perhaps, is when the

Dreamer joins the chase. "Who is hunting here?" he asks of a fellow who is leading a hound in a leash. "Sir," replies the huntsman, "it is the Emperor Octavian." "Good enough!" is the Dreamer's only comment, "let us make haste!" This is surely like a dream. There is no surprise at the news — no question who the Emperor Octavian is, or how he happens to be in that vicinity. Another point concerns the Dreamer's horse. What becomes of it after the hunt? We suddenly find the Dreamer on foot, walking away from the tree at which, though he has not said so, he has taken up his station, and he never thinks of his horse again. This, too, is very like a dream. Then there is the little puppy that has followed the hounds in its helpless fashion, and is now astray in the woods. It comes up to the Dreamer, and fawns upon him as if it knew him, but runs away when he would take it in his arms, and leads him down a grassy ride into the depths of the forest. Like the horse, the puppy drops out of the Dreamer's vision as other objects appear. Thus, we all remember, do dreams behave.

I do not contend that Chaucer carried out his dream-psychology in a thoroughgoing and consistent manner. That would have destroyed the continuity required in a narrative. But assuredly, in various details, he brought the experi-

ences of the Dreamer, with admirable art, near
to the actual phenomena of the dream-life.

Never was there a more conventional situation — a dream, a paradise of trees and flowers
and birds, a lamenting lover, an incomparable
lady. We who wander through the middle ages
have seen and heard it all a hundred times. Yet
somehow the conventions are vitalized. The
artificiality of the situation is merged and lost in
the illusions of dreamland, which here are genuine illusions, since the dream is really like a
dream. Two typical figures — the lover who
sighs in vain, and he who has loved and lost —
have come to life. First, the Dreamer, — innocent, helpless, childlike, a veritable John-a-
dreams, — joining a dream-hunt which comes to
naught, pursuing a little dog which disappears,
and finding under a tree a mourning knight
whom he cannot comprehend. And there are
greetings, and questions, and half-understood
replies. The Dreamer has the curiosity of a
child, and a child's yearning to comfort his in-
comprehensible elders. The knight has sought
solitude, but a child has stormed his fortress, a
grown-up child, who speaks the language of the
knight's own world. And the knight talks to the
Dreamer in transparent riddles, playing with his
own sorrow; he can confide in him all the better
for not being understood. And the dream be-

haves like a dream. Things grow clearer and clearer, until there is the shock of perfect revelation: "She is dead, I tell you! Can't you see what I mean?" "Is that your loss? By God, I am sorry for you!" The intrusion of reality marks the moment of waking. "A bell strikes twelve! Do I hear it in my dream, or is it the clock in the tower? Ah! I am awake, and here is my book of Ceyx and Alcyone still in my hand!"

The Book of the Duchess, with all its defects, is a very beautiful poem. There is a haunting charm about it that eludes analysis, but subdues our mood to a gentle and vaguely troubled pensiveness. The mind is purged, not by the tragedy of life, with its pity and terror, but by a sense of the sadness which pervades its beauty and its joy. Ours is a pleasant world of birds and flowers and green trees and running streams, and life in such a world is gracious and desirable, and nothing is so good as tender and faithful love, which is its own reward. But the glory of it all is for a moment. Alcyone prayed to Juno to send her a dream, that she might know whether her long-absent husband was alive or dead. And the drowned Ceyx came while she slept, and stood at her bed's foot, and bade her bury his body, which was cast up on the shore:—

> "And farewel, swete, my worldes blysse!
> I praye God youre sorwe lysse.
> To lytel while oure blysse lasteth!"

Now this thought — that life and love and happiness are transitory — is not, with Chaucer, a commonplace reflection, with which he has only a concern that is conventional and impersonal and external. Nor is it, again, a dogma of experience, to which he has dispassionately adjusted his philosophic scheme. It is an element in his nature: it beats in his heart, and flows in his veins, and catches in his throat, and hammers in his head. All men are mortal, no doubt, but seldom do we find one in whom mortality is a part of his consciousness. And such a man was Chaucer — yet so sound of heart, so sane and normal, so wholesome in his mirth, so delighting in the world and in his fellow-creatures, that no less a critic than Matthew Arnold, speaking with limited sympathy and imperfect comprehension, would exclude him from the fellowship of his peers on the strength of a formula, because he "lacked high seriousness." Whether Chaucer saw life whole, I do not know. One thing I know — he saw it steadily.

III

THE HOUSE OF FAME

CHAUCER'S Period of Transition, as defined in my first lecture, falls between his first Italian journey (in 1373) and the writing of the Palamon and Arcite or the Troilus, whichever of these two works came first. In this period he was reading and assimilating Italian poetry, was achieving emancipation from French fashions under its guidance, was "finding himself," was getting ready for the full exercise of his native genius. His leisure was scanty, and he read far more than he wrote, enlarging his knowledge on every side. In particular, he gave much time to the Latin classics, which must share with Dante and Petrarch and Boccaccio the honor of setting him free from the bonds of French convention.

The chief concrete product of this interval of rapid and virile development was the House of Fame, a poem not only of sufficient merit in itself to approach the rank of a masterpiece, but also in the highest degree remarkable for what it indicates. In design it is ambitious, far beyond anything that Chaucer had heretofore attempted or conceived. In substance, it is a kind of epitome of the author's knowledge and culture in science and art and philosophy, in French and Italian and Latin. It is composed, in small and great, with astonishing virtuosity. It is full of spirit and originality, and instinct throughout with conscious power.

The House of Fame is divided into three Books. The first is an introduction; the second describes the poet's marvellous journey through the upper air; the third gives an account of Fame's palace, with its surroundings and adjuncts, and of what is to be seen and heard in her domain.

The prologue to the First Book consists of two distinct parts, the Discussion of Dreams and the Invocation. Both will repay our study.

The Discussion begins with the pious wish, "God turne us every drem to goode!" but instantly flies off at a tangent in a characteristic disclaimer. The poet can make nothing of dreams, either as to their causes or their significance. Some of them appear to be mere fancies; others are oracles, revealing what is to come. The causes he finds particularly obscure and confusing. Are dreams merely reflexes of a man's own temperament? Or do they spring from physical fatigue and mental weariness, the result, perhaps, of fasting, sickness, imprison-

ment, over-study, devout contemplation, or, in
the case of lovers, of "the cruel life they lead"?
Do spirits put dreams into our heads? Or, finally,
has the soul so perfect a nature that it foresees,
in slumber, what is to happen to us, but in symbols only, which our gross bodies forbid us to interpret? "I know not," cries the poet, "nor do
I care to risk an ignorant guess!" And so he reverts to the prayer with which he began: "May
the Holy Rood grant us a favorable issue for
all our dreams!" and passes to his conclusion:
"For nobody, I believe, ever had so wonderful
a dream as I had on the tenth of last Decem-
ber. I will repeat it to you, as exactly as I can
call it to mind." The whole discussion, we note,
leads up to this final announcement, and works
as a powerful stimulus to the reader's curiosity.
In pure technique it is a little masterpiece, for
the substance of it is run into one long, eager,
and breathless sentence, extending to more than
fifty verses.

Equally remarkable is the pervasive air of
ironical detachment. This "sticks fiery off indeed" when one compares the Romance of the
Rose, in its exordium, of which Chaucer's is a
kind of antiphrastic counterpart: — "Many men
say that dreams are nothing but lies; but I am
sure, for my part, that some of them are true.
Such was the dream that I myself had when I

was nineteen years old; for it was all fulfilled in due season." The irony which prompts Chaucer to disclaim all knowledge of the philosophy of dreaming, becomes from this time forward a characteristic feature of his narrative method. We may infer, if we like, that it corresponds with a fact of his temperament. There is a curious relation between this ironic spirit in the House of Fame and the naïveté of the dreamer in the Book of the Duchess. Both poems belong in some sort to the genre of the Old French vision of love. In the Duchess, we have seen Chaucer applying the conventions of this genre to a highly original purpose, the writing of a personal elegy. In the House of Fame he is applying them to an entirely different but equally original end — a humorous survey of the whole world of mortal endeavor. There the mood was to be pathos; here it is to be high-spirited fun, though with a serious implication. There the dreamer was a fictitious character. Here he is certainly the poet himself; for the wise Eagle, whose acquaintance we shall make in a moment, calls him distinctly "Geoffrey."

It is no accident that in the Invocation that follows Chaucer puts up a prayer to Morpheus. He is thinking of the Book of the Duchess. There the god, of whose existence he was so surprised to learn, had served him well in sending him a dream. In other words, the Book of the Duchess had been favorably received; it had established Chaucer's reputation as a truly original poet, not merely as a clever translator from the French. So, therefore, he invokes the God of Sleep to help him to make good use of this dream also, which is far more wonderful than the former — indeed, the most marvellous that ever man had. And he attaches to his prayer a curse upon all hostile or malicious persons who shall make light of his work or attack it in any way: "Send them bad dreams, O Lord, and worse fulfilments!" A perfect nightmare of an imprecation!

We must not take this outburst, which is jocose to the verge of extravagance, as indicating that Chaucer had suffered from the critic's serpent tongue. No irresponsible indolent reviewers infested the English court. It is, in substance, a pure convention; Chaucer got the idea from the Anticlaudianus, which he had just been reading. But he has turned the convention, as usual, to his own purposes. Under cover of his irony, he is proudly self-assertive. He knows that the House of Fame is the best thing he has ever seen in the vernacular, and well worthy of immortality. He defies his readers not to like it, for he is sure they cannot help themselves. And so the dream begins.

Chaucer finds himself, with no tiresome pre-

liminaries of travel, in a huge temple of glass,
which he recognizes instantly as dedicated to
Venus. There is no living creature in the temple,
but the whole story of the Æneid is represented
on the inner wall, and Chaucer recounts it at
some length. We are to imagine an elaborate
series of painted scenes, each explained by a title
or legend, which in some cases must have run to
several lines.

This summary of Virgil's epic is in no sense
digressive, nor is it merely a decoration. Wall-
paintings are, to be sure, a familiar feature in
love-visions, but Chaucer once more applies the
convention in a novel way, and with a definite
artistic purpose. The Æneid, as he here con-
ceives it, is not the epic of Rome; it is the epic of
Venus. Her control is affirmed at the outset of
Æneas's wanderings, is emphasized continually,
and is reasserted, with a prayer, at the end: —

> How, mawgree Juno, Eneas,
> For al hir sleight and hir compas,
> Acheved al his aventure,
> For Jupiter took of hym cure
> At the prayer of Venus, —
> *The whiche I preye alwey save us,*
> *And us ay of oure sorwes lyghte!*

Thus we have the effect of a service in the empty
temple, with hymns and petitions, and with a
closing ascription of all praise to the power that

governs both gods and men. In this regard, the proportions of Chaucer's summary, which have been criticised, are easy to defend. He includes, it is true, the entire Æneid, but he gives to the story of Dido twice as many verses as to all the rest of the epic. In a word, he has completely shifted the emphasis, to serve his turn. A mere episode has become the substance of the story.

Chaucer has never visited this temple before; but he supposes, of course, that the region is inhabited, and goes out at the wicket, hoping to fall in with somebody to tell him where he is. To his consternation, he finds himself in a boundless waste of sand, a veritable Lybian desert, with no living being in view; and he raises his eyes to heaven and prays Christ to save him from "phantom and illusion." As he gazes devoutly upward, he catches sight of a great soaring eagle, with feathers of gold, hard by the sun, but, so it seems to him, descending somewhat toward this earth.

Here, with the close of the First Book, the introduction ends, and the action of the poem begins. The mighty golden bird swoops down upon the poet, seizes him without alighting, and bears him up to a monstrous height, so rapidly that he loses consciousness and lies a dead weight in the eagle's talons.

Before we accompany Chaucer in his aërial flight, which is the subject of the Second Book, we must dwell for a moment on Book First, which is the introduction. For the theory of ten Brink is a lion in the path. In the House of Fame, according to this eminent scholar, we are concerned with an allegorical picture of Chaucer's life and of what may be called his literary situation. If ten Brink is right at this point, he may or may not be right in his development of the theory; but if he is wrong here, we need harass ourselves no further with his interpretation.

Manifestly, we are bound to take account of the readers whom Chaucer had in mind. If we ignore these, and their stock of ideas, derived in large part from the French poetry of the thirteenth and fourteenth centuries, we shall make a mistake akin to that of reading Shakspere in forgetfulness of the Elizabethan audience. Great poets, no doubt, address themselves to posterity; and posterity is free to interpret them, for its own comfort and inspiration, in any terms that it finds useful. But they address themselves, in the first instance, to their immediate contemporaries. They may be for all time ultimately, but that is by virtue of the eternal nature of the things that really matter in human life. What Chaucer meant to his contemporaries is, then, a

pertinent question. It stands at the threshold.
If there is an inner shrine, we must enter it
through the portal of the obvious.

To ten Brink, the temple of glass is a figure
for the " charmed circle of poetry in which Chaucer lives under the spell of his study of the great
masters." The paintings on the wall are "those
pictures of life which he sees in his beloved
authors, and which serve as the sole intermedi-
aries between him and the world of men." The
sandy desert is "the loneliness that encompasses
him whenever he ventures beyond the four walls
of his little book-room."

Now these sentimental equations, we must
frankly admit, are quite unlike anything that
Chaucer's contemporaries would have gathered
from the story. The announcement at the outset,
that he is to tell them a dream — accompanied
as it is by a discussion of dreams which recalls
the exordium of the Romance of the Rose, the
most popular of all poems with the courtly circle
of the time — meant to them, undoubtedly, that
they were to hear one more variation on the
favorite theme of the love-vision. And this idea
was confirmed when they found the poet in a
Temple of Venus, admiring a love-tale painted
on the walls. The emptiness of the temple would
not surprise them, or lure them to far-fetched
guesses at a hidden meaning. There was nothing

odd in strolling into an empty church, when it
was not the hour of service, and looking at the
works of art. Nor were they surprised at the
painted walls; for such things were common in
real life, and had become a familiar convention
in the genre. They felt, therefore, — these fortunate knights and ladies of the middle ages, — no
such temptation as besets us ingenious moderns
to apply the temple, or the lack of worshippers,
or the poet's interest in the decorations, to anything in the actual circumstances of Chaucer's
life, or to his relations, good or bad, with the
world about him.

Moreover, if we scrutinize the supposed allegory a little, we shall perceive its ineptitude.
The temple in which Chaucer finds himself is
quite unfamiliar to him. He infers that it is dedicated to Venus, because he sees portraits of her
and Cupid, but he has no idea in what country it
is. Indeed, he leaves the building in the express
hope of discovering somebody who can answer
this question.

> When I had seen al this syghte
> In this noble temple thus,
> "A, Lord!" thoughte I, "that madest us,
> Yet sawgh I never such noblesse
> Of ymages, ne such richesse,
> As I saugh graven in this chirche;
> But not wot I whoo did hem wirche,
> Ne where I am, ne in what contree.

But now wol I goo out and see,
Ryght at the wiket, yf y kan
See owhere any stiryng man,
That may me telle where I am."[1]

Obviously, this unknown temple cannot stand
for Chaucer's habitual literary studies, and the
desert for his loneliness outside his book-room.
If so, we must infer that he used to go into the
London streets to ask the passers-by what his
own studies were, and that he felt disappointed
when no one could enlighten him. Moreover, the
sandy desert affects Chaucer not with a feeling of
personal lonesomeness, but with alarm. He is
lost in a desolate land, and there is no one to tell
him which way to go. What he needs is not sympathetic companionship, but direction: a finger-
post would console him as well as a man. In a
panic he prays Christ to save him "from phantom and illusion." He fears that he is taking
leave of his wits, or that he has wandered into
some enchanted region, like the knights errant in
romances. His suspicions embrace not only the
desert, but the marvellous temple, which now
seems equally uncanny. Such, plainly, is the situation, — certainly not interpretable in the
terms proposed by ten Brink.

In short, all attempts to read personal allegory
into the First Book of the House of Fame break

[1] Verses 468-479.

down completely when tested by comparison
with the actual narrative. And there is no neces-
sity to have recourse to personal allegory. The
temple and the desert are simply devices to transport the poet into the fantastic regions of dreamland, where the eagle can swoop down upon him
conveniently: Jove can hardly send his bird to
the custom house, or to Chaucer's city lodgings.
We are now dispensed, I should hope, from following the allegorical school in its further explor-
ations, and equating the huge eagle that bears
Chaucer aloft with "philosophy," or "poetic
genius," or "productive Phantasie." The attempt would only induce that state of mental
confusion which Chaucer himself experienced in
the eagle's talons:—

> "O God!" thoughte I, "that madest kynde,
> Shal I noon other weyes dye?
> Wher Joves wol me stellyfye,
> Or what thing may this sygnifye?
> I neyther am Ennok, ne Elye,
> Ne Romulus, ne Ganymede,
> That was ybore up, as men rede,
> To hevene with daun Jupiter,
> And mad the goddys botiller."

Chaucer evinces a wide and exact acquaintance with the aërial or celestial flights of many
personages, sacred and profane. In the verses
quoted he declines to identify himself with Enoch
or Elijah, with Romulus or Ganymede. Some-

what later he refers to the story of Dædalus and Icarus, to Scipio's Dream, and to the extraordinary aviation of Alexander the Great; he remembers Boethius and the flight of Thought, "with feathers of Philosophy," above the elements; he cites the Anticlaudianus, in which Prudentia rides through the sky in a car, with Reason as her charioteer. Greatly daring, after the mediæval manner, even to the edge of blasphemy, he allusively compares himself to Saint Paul in Second Corinthians: —

> Thoo gan y wexen in a were,
> And seyde, "Y wot wel y am here;
> But wher in body or in gost
> I not, ywys; but God, thou wost!"[1]

"Whether in the body, I cannot tell; or whether out of the body, I cannot tell: God knoweth."

The inference is unescapable: "Men have soared above the clouds at divers times and in sundry manners and have seen amazing sights. Some of these celestial journeys have been literal, others by way of allegory, still others in the rapture of a vision through the grace of God. I cannot classify my own experiences. All I know is, that I was dreaming; and, as I have told you, I am ignorant of the causes of dreams, and by no means expert in reading their signification. My eagle was Jove's messenger. He carried me

[1] Verses, 979–982.

without an effort, though I am no light weight. He astonished me by his powers as a mind-reader. There were no limits, so it seemed, to his knowledge, and he was uncommonly generous in imparting it." How idle it is, in the face of this exultant and characteristic irony, to rummage for the eagle's prototype in the junk-shops of antiquity, or to guess at what he typifies, as if he were a riddle with a specific answer! The office of the eagle in the economy of the poem is simple and unambiguous. Chaucer is to visit the Palace of Fame. It is situated, so Ovid says, at the central point

> inter terrasque fretumque
> caelestesque plagas, triplicis confinia mundi.[1]

> Hir paleys stant, as I shal seye,
> Ryght even in myddes of the weye
> Betwixen hevene, erthe, and see.[2]

He needs a conveyance. Jove's bird, decked with a feather or two from Dante, stands ready to perform this service at the god's command. But there is much that Chaucer needs to learn about his destination, and there are strange sights along the aërial road. A cicerone, then, is likewise requisite, and the poet has the happy thought of letting the eagle supplement the function of carrier by assuming also the rôle of guide, philosopher,

---

[1] Met., xii. 39-40.   [2] House of Fame, 713-715.

and friend. There is nothing particularly remarkable about this device, for guiding animals
who can talk are common enough in popular
story; but one cannot sufficiently admire the results of the combination. These are — to be cate-
gorical — a character, a situation, and a dialogue, quite unified in their total impression, yet
indescribable except in contradictory terms.
The art is the same that Chaucer used, much
later, in his mock-heroic masterpiece of the Cock
and Fox. Chanticleer and Pertelote, when they
converse, are human beings, a lord and his lady,
with characters as true to human nature as that
of Harry Bailly or the Wife of Bath. Yet, in a
moment, when we are almost forgetting that
they are barnyard fowl, a touch brings back the
reality, — the beams on which they roost, or the
corn of wheat, or the lovely scarlet red about
Dame Pertelote's eyes, or the diet of worms, or
"Pekke hem up right as they growe, and ete
hem in!"

The Second Book is taken up with an account
of Chaucer's wonderful journey through the
heavens to the Palace of Fame. Through it all,
Chaucer is quite passive, having, indeed, nothing
to do but to keep still. The admirable eagle does
all the talking. He is a most interesting character, and appeals especially to me and my academic brethren. For the eagle is a born lecturer,

particularly strong in popular science. He owes
his knowledge, of course, not to books, but to
exceptional facilities for observation. These,
unfortunately, are enjoyed in equal measure by
his associates at Jove's court. Now, at length,
he has buttonholed or kidnapped an auditor.
Chaucer lies helpless in the lecturer's talons, in
no condition to protest or disagree; and the
learned eagle holds forth, with all the gusto of
long repression. He shows the exuberance of an
autodidact and the condescending omniscience
of a discoursing specialist. Chaucer, who has no
wish to be dropped, is not contentious: he replies in monosyllables, with a meek yes or no, as
the occasion requires. His reticence is not dimin-
ished by the alarming discovery that the eagle
can read his thoughts! This one-sided conversation lasts throughout the aërial journey, and is
intensely amusing.

The eagle, having felt the pulse of Chaucer's
heart with one talon, to make sure that he has
recovered consciousness, begins with a much-
needed explanation, which includes the famous
passage describing the poet's retired and studious life. "Jupiter has taken pity on thy long
service in making books and songs and ditties in
honor of Love, in spite of Love's disregard of
thee. And he also considers thy lack of all
tidings of Love's folk.

"Wherefore, as I seyde, ywys,
Jupiter considereth this,
And also, beau sir, other thynges;
That is, that thou hast no tydynges
Of Loves folk yf they be glade,
Ne of noght elles that God made;
And noght oonly fro fer contree
That ther no tydynge cometh to thee,
But of thy verray neyghebores,
That duellen almost at thy dores,
Thou herist neyther that ne this;
For when thy labour doon al ys,
And hast mad alle thy rekenynges,
In stede of reste and newe thynges,
Thou goost hom to thy hous anoon;
And, also domb as any stoon,
Thou sittest at another book
Tyl fully daswed ys thy look,
And lyvest thus as an heremyte,
Although thyn abstynence ys lyte."[1]

"For these reasons, Jove has sent me to bear thee to the House of Fame, where thou canst hear every sort of love-news." And the eagle specifies the different kinds of tidings at some length and with inimitable vivacity; for, though a lecturer, he is far from being a bore. He winds up with a question: "I suppose this account of mine seems scarcely credible?" "Not credible at all," replies the poet with docility, for he knows that this is the answer expected. "Why so?" cries the eagle, delightedly. "Because I cannot understand how all these reports should be

[1] Verses 641–660.

brought to Fame's house from every quarter of the world," Chaucer answers, once more playing into his interlocutor's hand. "That is precisely what I can explain to you," rejoins the golden-feathered lecturer, now in the best of spirits. And then comes a long discourse on sound-waves, ending with a palpable bid for a compliment:—

> "Telle me this now feythfully,
> Have y not preved thus symply,
> Withoute any subtilite
> Of speche, or gret prolixite
> Of termes of philosophie,
> Of figures of poetrie,
> Or colours of rethorike?
> Pardee, hit oughte the to lyke!
> For hard langage and hard matere
> Ys encombrous for to here
> Attones; wost thou not wel this?"
> And y answered and seyde, "Yis."[1]

"Aha!" cries the eagle, in eager self-appreciation, and with an air of generous patronage:—

> "A ha!" quod he, "lo, so I can
> Lewedly to a lewed man
> Speke, and shewe him swyche skiles
> That he may shake hem be the biles,
> So palpable they shulden be."

Note this "shake them by the bills." It is like "pekke hem up" in the language of Dame Pertelote. This is a learned lecture, but the

[1] Verses 853–864.

eagle, after all, is a bird, and here he drops unexpectedly into the bird-idiom. This is excellent humor and first-rate psychology. "Haow?" said Dr. Holmes's theological student at the breakfast table, in a moment of abstraction, reverting to the vernacular of his rustic forefathers.

Satisfied with Chaucer's appreciation of his didactics, the eagle inquires how his charge is feeling. "Well," replies the poet, laconically. He is then bidden to look down at this earth, of which he gets an excellent bird's-eye view. Soon, however, they have risen to such a height that nothing terrestrial is any longer discernible, and the eagle directs his pupil's gaze upward to the galaxy and the signs of the zodiac. Presently even these "airish beasts" are below them. Their destination is nigh at hand, but the eagle sees a chance for one more lecture. He inquires whether Chaucer wishes any instruction in astronomy: —

"Wilt thou lere of sterres aught?"

But the poet, though much pleased with his instructor, has had almost enough. "Nay," is his unexpected answer, "I am too old for such learning." The eagle is comically insistent. "I would have told you their names," he suggests, "and also the names of the constellations."

"Never mind," says Chaucer, encouraging no
further exposition. The eagle is true to his
character: "You are wrong;" he declares,
"such information will be useful when you read
poetry." Chaucer proves a bit recalcitrant. He
has recovered his poise, and has courage enough
to argue: "No matter! I am willing to trust the
writers who deal with this subject. Besides, the
stars are so brilliant that my eyes would suffer."
"Perhaps you are right," says the eagle, who
realizes that there are limits to the patience of
the most submissive audience.

They arrive in Fame's precincts, and Chaucer
is set down in a street, safe and sound, and bidden to follow the road and he shall come to the
House of Fame. Feeling solid ground underfoot,
he suddenly gets back both his tongue and his
natural curiosity, and begs the eagle to explain
the noises that proceed from the palace. This
question is the eagle's best reward for his forbearance in the matter of an astronomical lecture. He explains, more briefly than usual but
with characteristic perspicuity, how the palace of
Fame is peopled: every speech that, by the laws
of sound already detailed, arrives at the building,
takes instantly the shape of the person who
uttered it. With this he bids Chaucer farewell,
promising to wait for him, and the poet makes
his way to the House of Fame.

Looking back on Book II, we observe that it
is not only written with extraordinary verve and
in the highest spirits, but that it is admirably
constructed. Everything is to the point and in
good proportion. The effect of a long, swift
journey through illimitable space is tellingly
brought out. Chaucer gradually recovers his
self-command as he gets accustomed to his
strange flight and better acquainted with the
bird of Jove. His recovery enables him to assert
himself when they near the journey's end, and to
head off the only lecture that threatened to be
tedious. One passage, the treatise on sound-
waves, is often regarded as a digression after the
true mediæval manner. In fact, however, the
passage is organically necessary to the realism
which the poet achieves in this the wildest of his
fictions, for it puts the whole structure upon a
basis of genuine science. After hearing it, Chaucer feels quite satisfied, and so do his readers,
that all the news of the world must make its way
to the Palace of Fame. Then, too, the account of
the laws of sound leads up directly to the explanation that every speech takes human shape when
it enters Fame's courts. We are thus prepared,
as Chaucer was, for the apparent reality of whatever is to be seen and heard in this region of
phantasmagoria. And, indeed, the verisimilitude
of the Third Book is complete.

Fame's House is an immense castle on the summit of a hill of ice, and nearly two hundred lines are devoted to its description. Within or without are all manner of minstrels, with jugglers, witches, and sorcerers: Orpheus is there, and the British Glascurion, and Marsyas, and Virgil's Misenus, and Circe, and Medea, and Simon Magus. There are many pursuivants and heralds, — everybody in short, who has to do with news or with the laudation of the rich and great. Fame herself sits enthroned in the hall, a grandiose and ever-shifting figure, according to the Virgilian description, and the Nine Muses are singing a hymn in her honor: —

"Heryed be thou and thy name,
Goddesse of Renoun or of Fame!"

Chaucer has the luck to be present when Queen Fame is holding audience. His account of the proceedings is a transparent allegory, of universal application. In fact, this allegory of Fame's treatment of her suppliants is an enormous expansion and development of the Virgilian truism which describes Fame as equally interested in the dissemination of falsehood and of truth. Chaucer's plan is a model of schematic precision. All men have some request to make of Fame, and the whole world comes to her throne, in nine separate companies. The treatment they receive exhausts the possibilities of arbitrary freakishness.

The first three companies are composed of meritorious persons who ask for good report as their appropriate reward. Fame treats them very differently. The first company is doomed to oblivion, their names shall die; the second company fares still worse, receiving world-wide slander instead of honor; the third gets what it asks, — the good renown that it deserves. The fourth and fifth companies pray that their merits may be forgotten: they have acted only for the glory of God. In one case, Fame grants the petition; in the other, she rejects it, and Æolus trumpets forth their praise to the ends of the earth. The sixth company are do-nothings, who have idled their life away, accomplishing neither good nor ill. Yet they are eager for reputation, and their prayer is heard. The seventh are also sluggards, who ask for the same favor, but receive derision and obloquy instead. The eighth company are villains: they ask for good renown, and are denied. The ninth consists of villains also, who exult in their crimes, and receive the evil reputation that they desire.

As thus condensed, the allegory seems cold and formal. In the poem, however, we forget the schematism in the liveliness of the narrative. The scene is brilliantly fantastic, yet somehow

real, with a piquant touch of the grotesque. The
conception is profoundly ironic, but leaves no
sting, for Chaucer's humor has unrestricted play,
and he is manifestly enjoying himself to the top
of his compass. The types of good or bad, of
modest piety or vainglorious wickedness, are
huge Collective Masses, who offer their petitions
to a gigantic Abstraction. But they are handled
as deftly as if everything were concrete and individual. Chaucer had not, to be sure, reached the
measure of his performance, but he was unques-
tionably in the full flush of matured power.

When Chaucer has had abundant opportunity
to note the freakish and perverse decrees of the
goddess, he is accosted by an affable by-
stander: —

> With that y gan aboute wende,
> For oon that stood ryght at my bak,
> Me thoughte, goodly to me spak,
> And seyde, "Frend, what is thy name?
> Artow come hider to han fame?"
> "Nay, for sothe, frend," quod y;
> "I cam noght hyder, graunt mercy,
> For no such cause, by my hed!
> Sufficeth me, as I were ded,
> That no wight have my name in honde.
> I wot myself best how y stonde;
> For what I drye, or what I thynke,
> I wil myselven al hyt drynke,
> Certeyn, for the more part,
> As fer forth as I kan myn art."[1]

[1] Verses 1868–1882.

Here eminent critics have unveiled a mystery. Chaucer, they imagine, depressed or disgusted because he has won no reputation commensurate with his merits, renounces fame altogether: it is a vain thing, a shadow which no man can grasp. I have no wish to follow the windings of this allegorical interpretation. If ever Chaucer exulted in his powers, if ever he felt the joy of writing, the thrill of fluent expressiveness, the rapture of an active intelligence working freely in a flexible and responsive medium, it was in the House of Fame. Nor is there a syllable in this little dialogue that suggests anything to the contrary.

"Who are you, friend?" asks the stranger. "Are you come hither in pursuit of renown?" "By no means, friend," the poet answers. "I came here for no such reason, — thank you very much! Let my name die." "What is your errand, then?" says the stranger. "I will tell you," the poet replies; and he gives a straightforward and accurate account of the purpose of his journey, — to learn new tidings, according to the eagle's promise.

Now what else, in all conscience, was Chaucer to say? He has not come hither in quest of reputation, and if he had, he must surely know, by this time, the futility of such an errand. His reply is the only one which a sensible man could have made, whatever his aspirations, after noting the arbitrary unreason of the goddess. "Let my name die" indeed! Why, he had just seen a whole troop of modest worthies who begged Fame to let them rest in obscurity, only to have their self-effacement rewarded by the widest publicity! Take the passage in its context, and the words of the poet lose all the esoteric significance that theorists attach to them. "Are you here for fame?" "No, thank you! I hope I am too wise for that, after what I have seen. I prefer to play the modest rôle and take my chances." I suppose there is no clearer utterance in all the works of Chaucer from end to end; but, like everything he writes, it must be taken in its context, with a feeling for the dramatic bearings of the situation. Character and circumstances should not be torn asunder.

Fame's hall of audience, though full of interest for the visitor, has disappointed him in one important respect. It has by no means kept the eagle's promise, for Chaucer has heard no tidings of lovers there. He confides his disappointment to his new friend, who straightway leads him out of the palace and points to an extraordinary structure close by, in a valley at the foot of the rock of ice. It is a vast house of wicker-work, shaped like a birdcage, and whirls about incessantly. Doors and windows stand open day and night, and tidings true and false pass in and out continually. The noise and confusion are terrific. This huge wicker cage is the rendezvous of all the rumors in the world, — their exchange, their clearing house, their bank of issue. Each flies forth again, modified, increased, compounded of false and true. It wings its way to Fame, who dwells in the castle nearby. She gives it a name that fits its disposition, grants it a period of life, and sends it off on its ambiguous errand.

Chaucer is eager to enter this House of Rumors. He catches sight of his eagle, perched demurely on a stone, and begs him to wait long enough to afford him an opportunity. It now appears that this is the precise destination of the whole journey. "Of course I will wait for you," says the condescending bird. "Jove has brought you hither to comfort you with tidings, and has instructed me to guide and assist you with all my might."

This speech of the eagle's is in the main a repetition of what he told Chaucer at the outset, and is therefore of prime importance for the understanding of the whole design. The mention of the poet's condition — he is heartbroken, languishing, "disesperat of alle blys" — attaches the story once more, in the plainest manner, to the traditional machinery of the visions of love. There is no basis whatever for a personal allegory. Neither the tedium of the custom house, nor the languor that results from over-application to books, has any status here. Least of all can we refer the passage to lonesomeness, to isolation in the crowd, or to the self-pity of neglected literary merit. The convention does not vary in any essential feature from that of the melancholy and sleepless lover in the Book of the Duchess. It is differently applied — to the purposes of a wonder-journey of intense ironical significance, not to those of an elegy — but in itself, and in its freedom from personal implications, it remains the same.

To test the point we may glance at the Arcadian machinery of the pastoral which is utilized by the poets in every conceivable fashion: — for elegy, as in Lycidas; for religious controversy, as in the Shepherds' Calendar; for courtly compliment, as in Herrick's verses on the birth of Prince Charles; for pure romance, as in Fletcher's Faithful Shepherdess, for abusive satire, as in Churchill's Prophecy of Famine; and for sportive humor, as in The Shepherd's Week of Gay.

The eagle has arranged a surprise for his charge, and incidentally for the reader too. Fame's Hall is not their final goal, though it is an important station in the itinerary. When Chaucer has seen enough of the goddess's power, there remains the House of Rumors, which will satisfy

his every wish and more than justify the promises
the eagle made him. But he cannot enter without the bird's assistance. The eagle picks him up
in his claws, which have lost their terrors by this
time, and darts in through an open window,
despite the rapidity of the revolutions.

Chaucer's experiences in the wicker house cannot be summarized. He had sinned against proportion in dwelling at such length on Fame's
Hall, but in the present scene there is not a super-
fluous line. The whole is conceived and executed
in a spirit of riotous humor, yet without extravagance and in perfect accord, in each detail, both
with the imagined situation and the underlying
allegory. The great magician rejoices in the gam-
bols of the spirits he has evoked, but they never
break loose from his control. Here are tidings
enough, and of every sort, "wingèd wonders,"
thousands of them. Yet there is plenty of room
for the purveyors of news; for men and rumors
can defy the laws of physics: both can be in the
same place at the same time.

> And, Lord, this hous in alle tymes,
> Was ful of shipmen and pilgrimes,
> With scrippes bret-ful of lesinges,
> Entremedled with tydynges,
> And eke allone be hemselve.
> O, many a thousand tymes twelve
> Saugh I eke of these pardoners,
> Currours, and eke messagers,

> With boystes crammed ful of lyes
> As ever vessel was with lyes.[1]

"Pilgrims, pardoners, and shipmen"! We can almost descry the Canterbury Tales in the distance.

But such long looks ahead are dangerous. They make "the sea and the aërial blue an indistinct regard." And we must not strain our eyesight, for here, at the very end of the poem, as it lies before us, truncated as it is but at a point not very far from the close, we reach the tidings of love at last. Chaucer hears a great noise in a corner of the building, where men are talking of love-tidings. Everybody ran thither, calling out, "What thing is that?" And they crowded together, and climbed up on each other's shoulders, and stamped on each other's heels; and then —

> Atte laste y saugh a man,
> Which that y [nevene] nat ne kan;
> But he semed for to be
> A man of gret auctorite. . . .

And so the poem breaks off, in the middle of a sentence apparently, and we are left to guess at the conclusion. Probably Chaucer finished the piece, and our manuscripts are defective. But that consideration avails nothing. We must use our wits — and with modesty; for, after all, we can do no more than cast the lots into the lap.

[1] Verses 2121–2130.

It seems evident that the "man of great authority" is to tell some first-rate piece of news concerning love. It cannot be a story out of a book, for that is not the kind of thing that Chaucer has been brought hither to hear, nor, if so, would it accord with the rumors and reports with which the house is filled. Most likely it is a contemporary affair, which would be of interest to the English court.

Whatever the news may have been, it cannot have taken long to tell, for the poem is nearing its end. Yet it must have been of sufficient consequence to come in effectively at the top of the climax. We must suppose, at all events, that the man told it, and that Chaucer listened. Then, no doubt, the poet woke up suddenly, as in the Book of the Duchess and the Parliament of Fowls. Any other conclusion would have departed too far from the regular programme of the love-vision, which Chaucer has applied to his purposes throughout, and which has determined the general structure of his work. To make the eagle carry him back to the sandy desert or the temple of Venus would be very tame. Going home after an adventurous excursion is always a dismal business.

Two features in the House of Rumors challenge our particular attention, its wicker framework and its vertiginous motion. Both are transparent symbols in the allegory, but neither, so far as we know, had ever been thus utilized before. Ovid, to whom Chaucer is here especially indebted, constructs his House of Fame out of sounding bronze, and does not make it whirl about. Was Chaucer inventing, or was he, as poets do, converting familiar material to novel uses? This is not a trivial question, — no mere frivolous conundrum for erudite and impertinent pedantry. Its answer, if we can find it, will extend our knowledge of Chaucer's horizon, both literary and actual, and may enlighten us not a little as to his methods as an artistic craftsman.

Fortunately the answer is at hand. The ancient houses of the Celts were made of wickerwork, and such structures were familiar sights in Chaucer's time, in Ireland, in the Scottish Highlands, and in Wales. Chaucer's erstwhile master, Prince Lionel, had lived in Ireland, and Chaucer knew scores of Englishmen who were familiar with Irish life. Wales was even nearer, and Chaucer was sufficiently impressed by the Bret Glascurion to assign him a conspicuous position among the harpers at the court of Fame. The poet knew plenty of Welshmen, and Sir John Clanvowe, who had hereditary possessions in Wales, was his friend and his poetical disciple. So peculiar a trait of Celtic life as these wicker houses was almost the first thing that would

strike an Englishman's eye. One odd feature of
the House of Rumors, then, is a transcript from
actual life. Chaucer the realist stands un-
masked before us.

But realism is only a fragment of life, or of
poetry. It needs its complement, or the world is
nothing but prose; and the complement of realism is romance. To debate their comparative
excellence is the very pedantry of literary criticism; to settle the question and fulminate against
the other side, is the crackling of thorns under a
pot. "Which came first," asked the ancient
schoolboy, "the hen or the egg?" Thanks to our
mediæval ancestors, we are well provided with
ammunition when the critics storm. We can always appeal with confidence — those of us who
refuse to sell our birthright — to Buridanus, to
the ass and the bundles of straw.

Chaucer wrote romances, — the Squire's Tale
is nothing else, — but he read romances first, all
that he could lay his hands on, whether French
or English. And it was in their enchanted regions
that he discovered the whirling castle, which the
errant knight can enter only by the help of a
guiding animal, — a creature that moves more
swiftly than the castle itself. The romances inherited this feature from the folk-tales, and in
some form or other, — the Symplegades, for
instance, or the door that slams constantly to

and fro, or the sky that shuts down suddenly like the jaws of a trap, — it goes back to the childhood of human thought.

Here, then, is the whole history of Chaucer's building. The real and the romantic (which, in the last analysis, is but an old, old way of interpreting phenomena) combine harmoniously in his imagination, which Ovid's allegory has set at work. The result is altogether original, something unattempted yet in prose or rhyme.

It remains to define, briefly, the relation of the wicker house to Fame's castle, for in that relation is involved the true meaning of Chaucer's parable.

Chaucer has by no means confused the two senses of the Latin *fama*. On the contrary, he has harmonized them. Fame, of course, is *reputation* or *renown*. Its substance or material, however, is nothing but *rumors*. The whirling wicker house, to which come all the words that are spoken on earth, is the factory or laboratory where rumors are compounded. These fly up to the castle close by, where Fame holds court. Thither all the world resorts, in continual throngs, to take whatever reputation the freakish goddess may assign them. This reputation is blown throughout the world by Æolus. It consists solely of the rumors just mentioned, for these are the wind which Æolus puffs from his trumpet. No wonder Chaucer declines to join the crowd of suppliants when he sees Fame's instability. He prefers to be silent and run his risks. Men in general are not so wise, or not so well-instructed.

The subject of the poem is, then, not Geoffrey Chaucer, but the human race. The poem is a humorous study of mankind from the point of view of a Ruling Passion.

I am glad the House of Fame is unfinished, for this gives me a chance to guess at the story that should conclude it. I have a very pretty theory, which, however, I shall not disclose, for I do not quite believe in it myself. Besides, I like to imitate Chaucer by stopping abruptly — checked, as perhaps he was, by the striking of the clock.

IV

TROILUS

CHAUCER is known to everybody as the prince of story-tellers, as incomparably the greatest of our narrative poets. Indeed, if we disregard the epic, which stands in a class by itself, I do not see why we should hesitate to call him the greatest of all narrative poets whatsoever, making no reservation of era or of language. His fame began in his own lifetime, and was not confined, even then, to the limits of his native country. It has constantly increased, both in area and in brilliancy, and was never so widespread or so splendid as at the present day. Besides, he is a popular poet, and this popularity — more significant than mere reputation — has grown steadily with the gradual extension of the reading habit to all sorts and conditions of men.

To most readers, however, Chaucer means only the Canterbury Tales; and even so, it is with but half-a-dozen of the pilgrims that they are intimately acquainted. This is manifest destiny, which it would be ridiculous to deplore: "What wol nat be, mot nede be left." Nor should we lament what Sir Thomas Browne calls "the iniquity of oblivion"; for oblivion has treated Chaucer generously. She has exempted enough of the poet's achievement to bring him popularity, which the conditions of his own time could neither afford nor promise, and she has spared besides, for such of us as care to read it, that masterpiece of psychological fiction

> In which ye may the double sorwes here
> Of Troilus in lovynge of Criseyde,
> And how that she forsook hym er she deyde.

The Troilus is not merely, as William Rossetti styles it, the most beautiful long narrative poem in the English language: it is the first novel, in the modern sense, that ever was written in the world, and one of the best. Authorship is a strange art: it is nearest akin to magic, which deals with the incalculable. Chaucer sat down to compose a romance, as many a poet had done before him. The subject was to be love; the ethical and social system was to be that of chivalry; the source was the matter of Troy; the material was Italian and French and Latin. His readers were to be the knights and ladies of the court, to whom the fame of the hero as a lover and a warrior was already familiar. Psychology it was to contain, or what passed for psychology in the mediæval love-poets, the analysis of emotion in terms of Chrétien de Troyes and the Roman de la Rose. Yet the work was not, in

Chaucer's intention, to be a romance precisely. He conceived it as what scholars then called a "tragedy," — though with a somewhat peculiar modification of the standard term. Tragedies described the malice of Fortune when she casts down men of high estate and brings them to a miserable end. This was to be a tragedy of love, and the fall of the hero was to be from happy union with his lady to the woe and ruin of her unfaithfulness. And so Chaucer took his pen in hand, and drew his quire of paper to him, and wrote a prologue.

The magician has marked out his circle, and pronounced his spells, and summoned his spirits. He knows their names, and the formulas that will evoke them, and the task that he shall require them to perform. And lo! they come, and there are strange demons among them, and when the vision is finished and the enchanter lays down his wand, he finds on his desk — a romance, to be sure, which his pen has written; a tragedy, in the sense in which he knew the word; a love-tragedy, with a background of the matter of Troy, and thousands of lines from Boccaccio, with bits of Benoit and Guido delle Colonne, and a sonnet of Petrarch's, and a section out of Boethius, and a closing prayer to the Christian God. Everything is as he had planned it. But, when he reads it over, he finds that he has produced a new thing. Nothing like it was ever in the world before.

The Troilus is a long poem, extending to more than eight thousand verses, but the plot is so simple that it may be set forth in a dozen sentences.

Troilus, Priam's son, and second in valor to Hector only, is a scoffer at love and lovers. On a high holiday, as he strolls idly about the temple of Pallas, heart-free and glorying in his freedom, his eye falls upon Cressida, daughter of Calchas. Her father has fled to the Greeks, to escape the doom of Troy; but Cressida remains in the city. She is a widow, young, rich, and of surpassing beauty. Troilus falls madly in love, but fears to reveal his passion. Pandarus, Cressida's uncle and Troilus' friend, coaxes the secret from him, and helps him with all his might. Cressida yields, after long wooing, and the lovers see naught but happiness before them.

One day, however, during an exchange of prisoners, Calchas persuades the Greeks to offer Antenor for Cressida, whom he fears to leave in the city of destruction. To resist is impossible. The lovers are parted; but Cressida promises to return in ten days, feeling sure that she can cajole her aged father. Her woman's wiles are fruitless: she must remain in the Grecian camp, where Diomede pays court to her assiduously.

He wins her at length, though not without her bitter grief at the thought of her unfaithfulness. Troilus is slain by Achilles.

This is the barest outline, but it suffices to show the simplicity of the story. The interest lies in the details, which are told with much particularity, and in the characterization, which is complex and subtle in a high degree. Readers who look for rapid movement and quick succession of incident, are puzzled and thwarted by the deliberation, the leisureliness, of the Troilus. The conversations are too long for them; they find the soliloquies languid; the analysis of sentiment and emotion and passion fails to keep their minds awake. But the Troilus is not a tale for a spare hour: it is an elaborate psychological novel, instinct with humor, and pathos, and passion, and human nature. Condensation would spoil it. Once yield to its charm, and you wish that it might go on forever.

Fate dominates in the Troilus. The suspense consists not in waiting for the unexpected, but in looking forward with a kind of terror for the moment of predicted doom. The catastrophe is announced at the outset: we are to hear of "the double sorrow of Troilus in loving Cressida, and how she forsook him at the last." Neither Troilus nor Cressida suspects what is to come; but we know all about it from the beginning.

There is no escape for anybody. We are looking on at a tragedy that we are powerless to check or to avert.

Chaucer himself conveys the impression of telling the tale under a kind of duress. Not, of course, that there is any literal compulsion. It is rather that he is entangled, somehow, in the subject, and that, since he has begun, he is in duty bound to finish his task.

> Syn I have bigonne,
> Myn auctour shal I folwen, if I konne.[1]

There is no weariness, as in some of the tales in the Legend of Good Women. His interest in the matter is intense, and it never falters. But he feels the burden of the ruin that is to come. At times he even seems to struggle against the fate which has allotted him so sad a duty. He would change the tale if he could, but he must tell the truth, though it is almost more than he can bear. He would actually impugn the evidence if that were possible: —

> For how Criseyde Troilus forsook,
> Or at the leeste, how that she was unkynde,
> Moot hennesforth ben matere of my book,
> As writen folk thorugh which it is in mynde.
> Allas! that they sholde evere cause fynde
> To speke hire harm, and if they on hire lye,
> Iwis, hemself sholde han the vilanye.[2]

---

[1] ii. 48–49; cf. i. 265–266, v. 1765–1769. [2] iv. 15–21.

So mightily is he stirred by Cressida's grief that
he would extenuate her guilt, or even excuse it
altogether, for sheer pity. She has been pun-
ished enough; and, after all, she was only a weak
woman, "tendre-herted, slydynge of corage."

> Ne me ne list this sely womman chyde
> Forther than the storye wol devyse.
> Hire name, allas! is punysshed so wide,
> That for hire gilt it oughte ynough suffise.
> And if I myghte excuse hire any wise,
> For she so sory was for hire untrouthe,
> Iwis, *I wolde excuse hire yet for routhe.*[1]

This extraordinary outburst works powerfully
upon our feelings. The case is hopeless. There is
no excuse but destiny, and destiny, though irresistible, cannot be pleaded even in extenuation.
Such is the law, and Chaucer bows to its everlasting antinomy, which, like Œdipus before him,
he does not pretend to reconcile.

Everywhere in the poem we find this idea of a
compelling destiny. It was Troilus' fate to love; [2]
he rode by Cressida's palace on "his happy
day," —

> For which, men seyn, may nought destourbed be
> That shal bityden of necessitee.[3]

"Swich is love," so Cressida moralizes, "and ek
myn aventure." [4] The oak topples over when it

[1] v. 1093–1099.   [2] i. 520.
[3] ii. 622–623.   [4] ii. 742.

receives "the fallyng strook." [1] Troilus apostrophizes the Parcæ, who settled his life for him before he was born: —

> "O fatal sustren, which, er any cloth
> Me shapen was, my destine me sponne." [2]

"Pleasure comes and goes in love," says Pandarus, "as the chances fall in the dice." [3] It was Fortune that cast Troilus down, "and on her wheel she set up Diomede," but Fortune is only the "executrix of weirds," and the influences of the stars govern us mortals as the herdsman drives his cattle: —

> But O Fortune, executrice of wyrdes,
> O influences of thise hevenes hye!
> Soth is, that under God ye ben oure hierdes,
> Though to us bestes ben the causes wrie. [4]

Most significant of all is the long meditation of Troilus on foreknowledge and freedom of the will in the Fourth Book. [5] This is from Boethius, and Chaucer has been as much blamed for inserting it as Shakspere for making Hector quote Aristotle. Doubtless the passage is inartistic and maladjusted; but it is certainly not, as some have called it, a digression. On the contrary, it is, in substance, as pertinent and opportune as any of Hamlet's soliloquies. The situa-

---

[1] ii. 1382.
[2] iii. 733–734.
[3] iv. 1098–1099.
[4] iii. 617–620.
[5] iv. 958 ff.

tion is well-imagined. Cressida is to be sent to
the Grecian camp. Parliament has so decided,
and resistance would be vain. Troilus, in despair,
seeks the solitude of a temple, and prays to
almighty and omniscient Jove either to help him
or to let him die. Destiny, he feels, has overtaken
him, for there seems to be no likelihood that
Cressida, if once she joins her father, will ever
return to Troy. What can he do but pray? Perhaps Jove will work a miracle to save him. And
as he meditates, in perplexity and distress, his
mind travels the weary maze of fate and free will,
and finds no issue, unless in the god's omnipo-
tence.

All this, no doubt, is un-Trojan; but that is
a futile objection. We have already accepted
Troilus as a mediæval knight and a mediæval
lover, and we cannot take umbrage at his pray-
ing like a man of the middle ages, or arguing with
himself in the mediæval manner. In details, to
be sure, the passage is open to criticism, and it
is undoubtedly too long; but in substance it is
dramatically appropriate, and it is highly significant as a piece of exposition. For Troilus finds
no comfort in his meditation. Whatever clerks
may say, the upshot of the matter is that "al
that comth, comth by necessitee." Whatever
is foreknown, must come to pass, and cannot
be avoided.

> "And thus the bifallyng
> Of thynges that ben wist bifore the tyde,
> They mowe nat ben eschued on no syde."

The fate which darkens the loves of Troilus
and Cressida is strangely intensified (in our ap-
prehension of it) by the impending doom of
Troy. This is no mere rhetorical analogue — no
trick of symbolism. Their drama is an integral
part of the great Trojan tragedy. They are
caught in the wheels of that resistless mechan-
ism which the gods have set in motion for the
ruin of the Trojan race. This is a vital, deter-
mining fact in their history, as Chaucer understands it, and he leaves us in no doubt as to its
intense significance. Calchas, we are told at the
outset, deserted Priam because Apollo had revealed the doom of Troy: —

> For wel wiste he by sort that Troye sholde
> Destroyed ben, ye, wolde whoso nolde.

And again and again we are reminded, as the
tale proceeds, of the inevitable outcome of the
ten years' war. Troilus is smitten with love
when he sees Cressida in the temple. It is the
great festival of Palladion, a relic, Chaucer calls
it, in Christian phrase, in which the Trojans put
their trust above everything. They were cele-
brating "Palladion's feast," for they would not
intermit their devout observances, although

the Greeks had shut them in, "and hir cite
biseged al aboute." When Pandarus finds his
friend plunged in a lover's grief, despairing of
ever winning the least favor from the lady he
has seen in the temple, the gibe that he casts
at him,—for the nonce, to anger him and arouse
him from his stupor—is an accusation of
cowardice:—"Fear, perhaps, has prompted
you to pray and repent, as at the approach of
death.

> "God save hem that biseged han oure town,
>   That so kan leye oure jolite on presse,
>   And bringe oure lusty folk to holynesse!"

When Pandarus first reveals to Cressida the
secret of Troilus' love, he approaches the subject carefully, so as not to startle her. "I could
tell you something," he cries, "that would make
you lay aside your mourning." "Now, uncle
dear," she answers, "tell it us, for love of God!
Is the siege over, then? I am frightened to death
of these Greeks."

> "As evere thrive I," quod this Pandarus,
> "Yet koude I telle a thyng to doon yow pleye."
> "Now, uncle deere," quod she, "telle it us
>   For Goddes love; is than th'assege aweye?
>   I am of Grekes so fered that I deye."[1]

Cressida felt the first thrill in her heart when she
saw Troilus riding through the street on his re-

---

[1] ii. 120–124.

turn from battle — his helm hewn to pieces, his shield pierced with Grecian arrows and cut and broken with the blows of swords and maces, — and the people were all shouting in triumph as he passed.

Always and everywhere we are oppressed by the coming doom of the city. This it is that prompts Calchas to beg the Greeks to give up their prisoner Antenor in exchange for Cressida. They need not hesitate, he argues; one Trojan captive more or less is nothing to them, — the whole city will soon be theirs. The time is near at hand

> "That fire and flaumbe on al the town shal sprede,
> And thus shal Troie torne to asshen dede."[1]

And, when Hector opposes the exchange, the Trojan people, in a riotous parliament, shout out their unanimous vote in its favor, and carry the day. Hector was right, though he did not know it for he was acting, not from policy or superior foresight, but from an honorable scruple: Cressida was not a prisoner, he contended; and Trojans did not use to sell women. And the people were fatally wrong. The "cloud of error" hid their best interests from their discernment; for it was the treason of Antenor that brought about the final catastrophe. It is, then,

[1] iv. 118–119.

the impendent doom of Troy that parts the lovers; and from this time forward, there is no separating their fate from the fate of the town.

When Cressida joins Calchas in the Grecian camp, she means to return in a few days. She has no doubt whatever that she can trick her father, and she has won Troilus over to her scheme. But she soon discovers that she has matched her woman's wit, not against her dotard father merely, but against the doom of Troy. No pretexts avail, not because Calchas suspects her plot, but because he knows that the city is destined to destruction. Nor does she dare to steal away by night, lest she fall into the hands of the savage soldiery. And finally, when Diomede wooes her, and gets a hearing, though little favor at first, his most powerful argument is the certain and speedy fate of Troy. He does not know that Cressida loves Troilus, — she tells him that she is heart-whole, but for her memory of her dead husband, — yet he cannot believe that so fair a lady has left no lover behind her, and he has seen her ever in sorrow. "Do not," he urges her, "spill a quarter of a tear for any Trojan; for, truly, it is not worth while. The folk of Troy are all in prison, as you may see for yourself, and not one of them shall come out alive for all the gold betwixen sun and sea!"

Thus, from first to last, the loves of Troilus

and Cressida are bound up with the inexorable
doom that hangs over the city. The fate of
Troy is their fate. Their story begins in the
temple of the Palladium; it is Calchas' foreknowledge and the people's infatuation that tear
them asunder; it is the peril of the town that
thwarts woman's wit, until Diomede subdues
the inconstant heart. The tragedy of character
grows out of the tragedy of situation.

Yet, after all, the Troilus is a tragedy of
character — profoundly moving and profoundly
ethical. We must study the characters, therefore,
— Troilus, Cressida, Pandarus.

There is little to be said of Boccaccio's Pandaro, and almost as little of his Griseida. Both
are vivid and lifelike, but neither shows any
subtlety in the delineation. Pandaro is young,
careless, and loose in his morals. He appeals
for his justification to the code of love, but only
in a perfunctory way. Griseida is frankly amorous, and her procrastination is quite *pro forma:*
it does not even amount to coquetry. Pandaro
sees through her pretences, and has slight reason for treating them with respect. Troilo is
hardly distinguishable from Pandaro, except
in his misfortunes. Both are simply young men
about town, with the easy principles of their
class. If they changed places, we should not
know the difference. The winning of Griseida

takes time, but requires slight craft or clever-
ness. No man in his senses could expect her to
be faithful.

Let us not minimize Chaucer's indebtedness
to Boccaccio. It is very great, in gross and in
detail. Without the Filostrato, the Troilus would
never have existed. But the characterization is
Chaucer's own.

Nothing can be more absurd than to describe
Chaucer's Troilus as a "lovesick boy." On the
contrary, he is a gallant warrior, second only
to the unmatchable Hector in prowess. And he
is wise withal, except in scoffing at the god of
love. To have brought down such a victim with
a single shaft is convincing evidence of the might
of the god. "Take warning, all ye haughty
gentlemen who think you are your own masters.
Love can subdue you when he will. Wisdom is
no protection against his assaults. History is
full of examples": —

> Men reden nat that folk han gretter wit
> Than they that han be most with love ynome.

Troilus is jeering at lovers at the very moment
when the god smites him: —

> "I have herd told, pardieux, of youre lyvynge,
> Ye loveres, and youre lewed observaunces,
> And which a labour folk han in wynnynge
> Of love, and in the kepyng which doutaunces;
> And whan youre prey is lost, woo and penaunces.

O veray fooles, nyce and blynde be ye!
Ther nys nat oon kan war by other be."

And with that word he gan caste up the browe,
Ascaunces, "Loo! is this naught wisely spoken?"
At which the God of Love gan loken rowe
Right for despit, and shop for to ben wroken.
He kidde anon his bowe nas naught broken;
For sodeynly he hitte hym atte fulle;
And yet as proud a pekok kan he pulle.[1]

Here Chaucer is in full conformity with the doctrines of the chivalric system, and we must accept
the convention before we try to interpret the
character of his hero. Nothing is more axiomatic,
in this system, than the irresistible nature of
love. The god is perfectly arbitrary. The will
of a man has nothing to do with the matter. You
can no more explain why one person falls in love
with another than why this fish comes into the
weir rather than that. Such is Chaucer's own
expressive comparison.[2]

The sufferings of Troilus are in complete
accord with the mediæval system. Lovers were
expected to weep and wail, and to take to their
beds in despair. It was likewise an article of the
code that they should be afraid to declare their
passion. Humility was one of the cardinal virtues
of the chivalric system. The lover must feel
convinced of his unworthiness; he must regard

[1] i. 197–210.   [2] iii. 33–35.

it as inconceivable that his lady should stoop to such as he.

Now all these dogmas are merely expressions, in language different from ours, of facts that no one challenges when couched in modern terms. To ignore them is impossible; to translate them into our conventions would be unendurably prosaic. We must understand them in their fourteenth-century attire, or refrain from judging the words or the actions of Chaucer's *dramatis personae.* The convention is only the costume in which emotion attires itself, and fashions change. If Garrick were to come back, and play Macbeth once more in knee-breeches and a tie-wig, should we take the clothes for the character? We are preposterous when we laugh at a mediæval hero for his love-madness. One would fancy that we never read the newspapers, or that (like Chaucer in the House of Fame) we had no tidings from our very neighbors. Give me forty-eight hours, and I will translate every mediæval symptom into modern journalese, and my version shall keep step with the daily records.

Such madness, indeed, makes a definite category among the kinds of insanity described by the old physicians whom Chaucer specifies as the masters of his Doctor in the Canterbury Tales. It is what Burton calls "heroical love."

The history of the term has very recently been traced by Professor Lowes in a masterly essay. It is the "lover's malady of Hereos" which the Knight mentions in his tale. There are two points at issue, the medical and the chivalric. What to the physician were symptoms — grief, pallor, sleeplessness, incessant unmotivated activity — became, in the chivalric system, duties—ideals of emotion which the true lover must live up to, and which the hypocrite takes pains to counterfeit.

Chaucer's mental attitude toward the whole phenomenon is at once sympathetic and ironical. He understood, for he was human, and human nature was, to him, the most interesting and moving subject in the world, — the only tangible thing, indeed, in a universe of mystery and thwarted endeavor. There is a God, who governs us, and to whom we must submit; but he is an object of faith. Human nature is the one thing that we can comprehend; and to comprehend, with Chaucer, was to sympathize, for he felt himself a part of all he saw. But Chaucer was also the supreme ironist, the kindly man of humor, with a touch of subtle melancholy which is essential in such a temperament. If we could imagine a being whose nature should be pure reason, how absurd we should all appear to him! "He that sitteth in the heavens shall laugh:

the Lord shall have them in derision." But, even to a mortal with keen perceptions, the everlasting tangle of humanity, in its frenzied pursuit of the unattainable, its undying hope, uninstructed by experience, is a fit subject for humorous contemplation. Otherwise, what shall one do but despair and die?

Cressida is as lifelike as Boccaccio's heroine, but far more complex. Griseida is elemental: her emotions are simple and straightforward, and involve no problems. But Cressida is marvellously subtilized, baffling alike to us and to herself. Quite as amorous as her prototype, she is of a finer nature, and has depths of tender affection that no Griseida could fathom. Her love for Troilus begins in that vague feeling of interest, with a touch of sentiment, which is the natural reflex of his love for her. Then, at the moment of destiny, he rides by her window, returning from battle, with the scars of conflict on his shield and helmet, amid the shouts of the exultant throng: —

> His helm tohewen was in twenty places,
> That by a tyssew heng his bak byhynde;
> His sheeld todasshed was with swerdes and maces,
> In which men myght many an arwe fynde
> That thirled hadde horn and nerf and rynde;
> And ay the peple cryde, "Here cometh oure joye,
> And, next his brother, holder up of Troye!"[1]

[1] ii 638–644.

Something stirs in her soul, — too indistinct
for expression, even in thought. It is still sentiment, not passion; but it affects her strangely,
so that she asks herself in gentle wonder, "Am I
under a spell?"

That to hireself she seyde, "Who yaf me drynke?"

Here Chaucer is very explicit, for he is determined not to be misunderstood. "This was no
sudden passion," he protests. "I do not mean
that she fell in love with Troilus all in a moment.
What I say is, that she began to like him, and
I have told you why; and thus, in time, and
by faithful service, he won her love, but in no
sudden way."

Now myghte som envious jangle thus:
"This was a sodeyn love; how myght it be
That she so lightly loved Troilus,
Right for the firste syghte, ye, parde?"
Now whoso seith so, mote he nevere ythe!
For every thyng, a gynnyng hath it nede
Er al be wrought, withowten any drede.

For I sey nought that she so sodeynly
Yaf hym hire love, but that she gan enclyne
To like hym first, and I have told yow whi;
And after that, his manhod and his pyne
Made love withinne hire herte for to myne,
For which, by proces and by good servyse,
He gat hire love, and in no sodeyn wyse.

Slowly, almost insensibly, under the sweet influences of the stars in their courses, sentiment develops into tender and passionate love. The passion is inconstant; it shifts from Troilus to Diomede: but the tenderness knows neither chance nor change.

This softness of affection is, in truth, the secret of Cressida's enduring charm. Troilus was never so dear as when she forsook him. "Men say," writes Chaucer, "that she gave her heart to Diomede, but I cannot tell. She was false, no doubt, for thus the record stands; but she grieved so piteously that I would excuse her sin, for very ruth, if that were possible!" She makes no defence at the bar of her conscience, — offers no plea in extenuation. Troilus is the truest lover woman ever had, and, in the very agony of her self-pity, looking forward to everlasting shame, she lauds his faithfulness, and vows to cherish his memory as long as she lives. Infinite is the pathos of her valediction: —

> But trewely, the storie telleth us,
> Ther made nevere woman moore wo
> Than she, whan that she falsed Troilus.
> She seyde, "Allas! for now is clene ago
> My name of trouthe in love, for everemo!
> For I have falsed oon the gentileste
> That evere was, and oon the worthieste!
>
> "Allas! of me, unto the worldes ende,
> Shal neyther ben ywriten nor ysonge

No good word, for thise bokes wol me shende.
O, rolled shal I ben on many a tonge!
Thorughout the world my belle shal be ronge!
And wommen moost wol haten me of alle.
Allas, that swich a cas me sholde falle!

"Thei wol seyn, in as muche as in me is,
I have hem don dishonour, weylaway!
Al be I nat the first that dide amys,
What helpeth that to don my blame awey?
But syn I se ther is no bettre way,
And that to late is now for me to rewe,
To Diomede algate I wol be trewe.

"But, Troilus, syn I no bettre may,
And syn that thus departen ye and I,
Yet prey I God, so yeve yow right good day,
As for the gentileste, trewely,
That evere I say, to serven feythfully,
And best kan ay his lady honour kepe"; —
And with that word she brast anon to wepe.

"And certes, yow ne haten shal I nevere;
And frendes love, that shal ye han of me,
And my good word, al sholde I lyven evere.
And, trewely, I wolde sory be
For to seen yow in adversitee;
And gilteles, I woot wel, I yow leve.
But *al shal passe*; and thus take I my leve."[1]

Everything passes, mutability is the order of the world; and what is so deceitful as her own heart? Yet she cannot quite despair. She has youth and beauty, and Diomede is a gallant knight. To him, at all events, she will be constant!

[1] v. 1051–1085.

"But syn I se ther is no bettre way,
And that to late is now for me to rewe,
To Diomede algate I wol be trewe."

Critics are strangely at variance in their judgment of Cressida. The confusion results from a failure to grasp, or to remember, the principles of courtly love. Under this code, there was nothing wrong in Cressida's yielding to Troilus. That, indeed, was a meritorious action. Her sin consisted solely in her unfaithfulness, in forsaking him for Diomede. On this point there cannot be the slightest doubt. Courtly love, however it may be adorned with flowers of rhetoric, was not platonic. Its doctrines were never thought to be reconcilable with Christian ethics. It had its own morality, in which fidelity was the highest virtue, infidelity the most heinous of crimes. How far this code was a mere convention, and how far it was reduced to practice by the ladies and gentlemen of the middle ages, is a long and troublous debate, into which we need not enter. The system was, at the very least, sufficient basis for a novel; for it commanded a theoretical acceptance and was closely connected with habits of conversation and various social amusements. The moral Gower, who was undeniably religious, adopted the code for literary purposes in his Confessio Amantis, with no thought of incongruity.

The theories of the chivalric code were known to Chaucer's readers, and they were immediately taken for granted on his announcement, in the proem to the First Book, that the Troilus is dedicated to love's servants. However correct their personal code of morals, they accepted the ethics of chivalric love for the purposes of this poem without demur, precisely as we in modern times accept the barbarous and outworn code of revenge when we read Hamlet. The lover must be violently affected by his passion. He must suffer torments and give way to bitter grief. Yet he should not utterly despair, for that would show lack of faith in the god. As for the lady, she should not scorn her suitor, but should regard his passion as entitling him to consideration. Her self-respect requires her to be distant, cold, and even cruel. She must not yield too easily; but if she finds her lover courteous, faithful, and discreet, she may properly return his love when he has proved his fitness for so great a reward.

These considerations clear up many difficulties. Chaucer's Cressida belonged to a social system which accepted the chivalric code. She knew its precepts well, and this knowledge is, so to speak, the background on which her thoughts and words and actions are all projected. She is not easily won, but her surrender is con-

scious and voluntary; for she is neither ignorant
nor unsophisticated. The dialect of chivalric
love is as familiar to her as it is to Pandarus, and
she is never cajoled by her uncle's high-flying
phrases. To regard her as an innocent girl, basely
tricked by a perfidious go-between, is to misconceive both the situation and the *dramatis
personae*. Pandarus uses plain language more
than once, and even his wiles are transparent
enough to one who understands the courtly doctrines. Cressida, though soft-hearted and of
a pliant disposition, is an uncommonly clever
woman, and she is mistress of her own actions.
Certainly she is in no sense the victim of a plot.
When Pandarus invites her to pay him a visit,
she asks, in a whisper, "if Troilus is there."[1]
Pandar lies, of course, but it is perfectly clear
that she does not believe his protestations. And
later, to clinch the matter, we have her answer
to Troilus: "Dear heart, if I had not yielded long
ago, I should not now be here."

> "Ne hadde I er now, my swete herte deere,
>   Ben yold, ywis, I were now nought heere!"[2]

She glories in her love, and her happiness is
unclouded by regret. Shame and repentance
would have been unintelligible terms. She has
acted in obedience to her own code, and our
ethical system has no status in the case.

[1] iii. 569.   [2] iii. 1210–1211.

Cressida, then, is not a victim, as some have thought. Just as little is she, as others hold, a scheming adventuress. This view of her character is, indeed, so patently erroneous as to need no refutation. True, she keeps her eyes open, and takes no leaps in the dark. She has also the excellent mental habit of looking at a subject or a proposition from several points of view. Finally, she is a lively conversationalist, the best company in the world. These are good traits, however, and, combined as they are with a tender and affectionate heart, an emotional nature, and a certain timidity in the face of possible danger, they vastly increase her feminine charm. It is ridiculous to accuse her of insincerity in her love for Troilus. To be sincere, it is not necessary to be either solemn or stupid. The allegation that she encourages Troilus because he is a prince, and with a view to securing his protection, — in a word, from selfish regard to her personal interests — rests upon a strange misunderstanding. When she turns her mind to these considerations of his rank and her own precarious position as the daughter of a traitor, she is merely seeking to justify to her reason the interest she is beginning to feel in her gallant lover, — for she knows full well that it may ripen into love. The subterfuges by which, at a later time, she expects to

induce her father to assent to her return, are
simply pathetic in their futility. They serve
the double purpose of proving her love for
Troilus, since Chaucer says they were well
meant, and of displaying the weakness of a
woman's wit (or a man's either, for that matter) when it sets itself up in opposition to the
decree of the gods.

Still another interpretation of Cressida's character finds that it deteriorates suddenly in the
latter part of the poem, and explains this change
either as the logical result of sin, or as the unsteadiness of Chaucer's portraying hand.

To all this, the answer is a flat denial, both
general and specific. First, there has been no
sin — that is, no sin against the god of love,
whose commandments alone are the ethics here
applicable. Let us test this judgment by an
hypothetical case. Suppose Cressida had assented to Troilus' plan to resist the parliament's
decree and had been slain in the insurrection.
Why, she would have been love's martyr, —
she would have won a place in the Legend
of Cupid's Saints! Sin begins when she wavers
in fidelity, when she lends an ear to the wooing of "this sudden Diomede." And secondly,
there is no deterioration; or, to take the other
point of view, there is neither inconsistency
nor unsteadiness in Chaucer's portrayal of his

heroine. As Cressida is at the beginning, such is she to the end; amorous, gentle, affectionate, and charming altogether, but fatally impressionable and yielding. Her strength of will is no match for her inconstant heart. " Tendreherted," Chaucer calls her, "slydynge of corage." The Filostrato is the tragedy of Troilus; Chaucer has made it the tragedy of Cressida also, — this "sely woman," who could not withstand her nature, but who was so sorry for her untruth that he would forgive her if he could. The record stands, punishment must follow; but there shall be no rebuking words from the judge who passes sentence.

> Ne me ne list this sely womman chyde
> Forther than the storye wol devyse.

Cressida is not a simple character, like the elemental Griseida of Boccaccio; but her inconsistencies are those of human nature. There is one Cressida, not two; or rather, there are two in one, — not a type, but an individual, unified by the interplay of her very contradictions.

This effect of complex unity in Cressida's character is heightened, with extraordinary subtlety, by a trait which I almost fear to touch, lest I blur its delicate clearness with a critic's clumsy finger. It is the trait of religious skepticism. Her father is Apollo's priest, but she has scant reverence for his sacred office, and little faith

in the revelations that the deity vouchsafes.
Oracles, she protests, are ambiguous always;
the gods speak ever in crafty double meanings,
telling twenty lies for one truth. Perhaps, indeed, there are no gods at all, save those that
shape themselves in the dark corners of man's
timid soul. "Primus in orbe deos fecit timor."

"Eke drede fond first goddes, I suppose."[1]

I am very anxious not to be misunderstood. This
is doubt, not dogma. Cressida is fighting with
fate, not laying down the law. Torn from her
lover by external forces that she cannot resist,
she swears to return, in vows that "shake the
thronèd gods," but it is not to the gods that she
trusts in her exigency. A woman's wit is to be
wiser than the powers that govern the world.

It is a very pregnant manifestation of Chaucer's feeling for the irony of life and circumstance when he makes Pandarus the exponent of
chivalric love. Here we must walk circumspectly.
Before attempting analysis of character, we
should determine externals; for it is as easy to get
Pandarus wrong as to misconceive the position
of Polonius in the Danish state.

Pandarus is a Trojan nobleman, next in rank,
it appears, to princes of the blood and on intimate terms with the whole royal family. He

[1] iv. 1408.

is the head of a powerful clan, which he offers
to rally to Troilus' assistance in preventing the
exchange of Cressida for Antenor.

Boccaccio's Pandaro is a young gallant, and
a cousin of Cressida's; Chaucer's Pandarus is her
uncle, and considerably older than Troilus. The
change is, of course, deliberate, and by its means
Chaucer is enabled to raise his Pandar from a
typical, though lifelike, figure to one of the
most remarkable of all comedy characters. We
must take care, however, not to exaggerate the
difference in age between the friends; for Troilus
is not a boy, and middle age in the fourteenth
century was ten years younger than it is to-day.
It will never do, with William Rossetti, to call
Pandar a "battered man of the world." He likes
to talk, and with good reason, for he is the very
demon of expressiveness. He has wit at will and
humor inextinguishable. Mankind has been his
study; life is his delightful privilege. His conversation is full of point and spirit, shifting continually from grave to gay, from game to earnest, easy, graceful, alert, never flagging, always
at the highest tension, but with no sense of
strain. Man of the world he is, assuredly, but
the world has not "battered" him. He is
gallant and high-spirited, himself a lover and
a servant of the god with all his heart. He
might even be a sentimentalist, if he were not

a humorist and a man of action. He is never more sincere than when he jests most recklessly. There is nothing cynical about him, except at times the turn of his epigrams.

This Pandarus, the arch-humorist, who preaches of the duties and the rewards of lovers like a devotee, has had no luck in his own affair. He has paid court for years to an obdurate lady, and his notorious sufferings have made him the laughingstock of his friends. Yet, despite his own miserable failure, he is radiant with optimism. "Many a man has served his lady for twenty years without so much as a kiss. Ought he, therefore, to fall into despair, or to abandon his allegiance to the god? No, no! He should rejoice that he can serve the dear queen of his heart, and he should count it a guerdon merely to serve her, a thousandfold greater than he deserves!"

"Thow mayst allone here wepe and crye and knele,—
But love a womman that she woot it nought,
And she wol quyte it that thow shalt nat fele;
Unknowe, unkist, and lost, that is unsought.
What! many a man hath love ful deere ybought
Twenty wynter that his lady wiste,
That nevere yet his lady mouth he kiste.

"What? sholde he therfore fallen in dispayr,
Or be recreant for his owne tene,
Or slen hymself, al be his lady fair?
Nay, nay, but evere in oon be fressh and grene

To serve and love his deere hertes queene,
And thynk it is a guerdon, hire to serve,
A thousand fold moore than he kan deserve."[1]

Pandarus bears his affliction with a jaunty
air; "a jolly woe" he calls it, "a pleasant sorrow"; and he never takes offence at jests. "Good
morning, uncle," says Cressida roguishly, "how
far have you come forward in the dance of
love?" "By Jove!" he cries, catching up the
trope, "I always go hopping along in the rear;
I cannot keep up with the other dancers!" We
must not refuse, however, to take his passion
seriously. Chaucer saw the danger, and he has
put the facts beyond the reach of doubt.[2]

Pandarus has the distinctive quality of the
pure humorist: he perceives the true comic element in himself, that is, in his own standing
toward his character and environment, his theories and his acts. He has the gift to see himself, not, perhaps, as others see him, but as they
might see him if they were Pandarus; and he is,
therefore, the object of his own sympathetic
amusement. Thus he is a rare but perfectly human compound of enthusiasm and critical acu-
men. To take him for a cynic is a pretty flagrant
piece of critical aberration.

Pandarus is Troilus' friend and Cressida's
uncle. This double relation is the sum and sub-

[1] i. 806–819.   [2] ii. 50–70.

stance of his tragedy, for it involves him in an action that sullies his honor to no purpose. Since Cressida is faithless, he not only labors in vain, but ruins his friend by the very success that his plans achieve. This humorous worldly enthusiast has two ideals, friendship and faith in love. To friendship he sacrifices his honor, only, it seems, to make possible the tragic infidelity of Cressida, which destroys his friend. The system of courtly love had neither comfort nor excuse for Pandarus. Though Cressida's love for Troilus was blameless, or even meritorious, under the code, yet that same code, in its inconsistency, held no justification for the go-between. And, after all, Cressida is not persuaded by Pandarus, but by her own temperament. She reads her uncle easily, and acts as she will, no matter what he may say. Herein consists the subtlest of all the ironies in this amazing document. "The fly sat on the chariot wheel, and cried, 'What a dust do I raise!'"

Pandarus is Troilus' friend. The middle ages liked to exemplify virtues and vices to the last gasp, as in the case of Griselda's patience, even if the conflict of duties was ignored. Pandarus, however, is too individual and lifelike to take sanctuary in a parable, though his conduct might well entitle him to some such refuge. It was an old theory, which Lælius repudiated with horror, that friendly devotion should know neither limit nor scruple: — *si voluisset, paruissem*. There was some excuse for this view in the middle ages, when men changed sides with a light heart and personal loyalty was much needed as a steadying element in politics and society. In Pandarus, no doubt, the ideal has gone astray in the application, but there is something pathetic in the intensity with which he errs. It is, in truth, the monomania of personal devotion, and that too on the part of a humorous ironist, who cherishes few illusions. "I have," he declares, "in true or false report, in wrong and right, loved thee all my life." One should remember, too, that he feared Troilus would die or go mad, and that the experience of every day proves that his fear, though we scoff at it as a literary convention, was by no means unreasonable. In his desperate fidelity to his passion of friendship, Pandarus cares nothing for himself. "Resist the king and the parliament," he cries, "and carry Cressida off in spite of their teeth. I will stand by you, though I and all my kindred shall be slain and lie dead, like dogs, in the street!"

"I wol myself ben with the at this dede,
Theigh ich and al my kyn, upon a stownde,
Shulle in a strete as dogges liggen dede,
Thorugh-girt with many a wid and blody wownde."[1]

[1] iv. 624–627.

This is not rhetoric; it is stark realism. Chaucer and all of his readers had seen slain men lying in the street like dead dogs.

From the beginning, the Troilus professes to be a poem in praise of the God of Love and in celebration of his wondrous powers. Chaucer is, so he avers, a mere outsider in such things; but he is the *servus servorum* of the divinity, and he hopes that his work may be of some use to Love's faithful disciples.

Troilus is a scoffer at first. He calls the devotees of the courtly system "fools," and the god of love "St. Idiot, the lord of fools." "Your order is well-ruled;" he cries in contempt, "you get not good for good; but scorn for faithful service." Later he becomes a convert to love's religion, and the great exemplar to all who worship the god. Cressida, at the very moment of renouncing him, calls him the most faithful of lovers; and "as true as Troilus" was a proverb for hundreds of years.

But, as we read on, we become aware that something is amiss. For there are no happy lovers in the story. Pandarus himself is a sufferer from unrequited affection; Œnone has been abandoned by Paris; Helen has brought the city to the edge of the abyss; Cressida is false to Troilus, and Diomede, we foresee, will scarcely be true to her.

The tone does not change. The faithful devotion of Troilus is represented as the highest of virtues, and the treason of Cressida as the most heinous of crimes, still from the point of view of the chivalric code. Yet we come more and more to suspect that Troilus was right in his first opinion; that the principles of the code are somehow unsound; that the god of love is not a master whom his servants can trust. And then, suddenly, at the end of the poem, when the death of Troilus has been chronicled, and his soul has taken its flight to the seventh sphere, the great sympathetic ironist drops his mask, and we find that he has once more been studying human life from the point of view of a ruling passion, and that he has no solution except to repudiate the unmoral and unsocial system which he has pretended to uphold.

"Such was the end of Troilus, despite his honor and his royal estate. Thus began his loving of Cressida, and in this wise he died at the hands of Achilles. O ye young men and maidens, in whom love grows with your growth, and strengthens with your strength, leave the vanity of the world and cast up the visage of your hearts to God! Set your love upon Christ, who died for love of you, for I dare well assure you that he will never betray the heart that trusts him."

Swich fyn hath, lo, this Troilus for love!
Swich fyn hath al his grete worthynesse!
Swich fyn hath his estat real above,
Swich fyn his lust, swich fyn hath his noblesse!
Swych fyn hath false worldes brotelnesse!
And thus bigan his lovyng of Criseyde,
As I have told, and in this wise he deyde.

O yonge, fresshe folkes, he or she,
In which that love up groweth with youre age,
Repeyreth hom fro worldly vanyte,
And of youre herte up casteth the visage
To thilke God that after his ymage
Yow made, and thynketh al nys but a faire
This world, that passeth soone as floures faire.

And loveth hym, the which that right for love
Upon a crois, oure soules for to beye,
First starf, and roos, and sit in heven above;
For he nyl falsen no wight, dar I seye,
That wol his herte al holly on hym leye.
And syn he best to love is, and most meke,
What nedeth feynede loves for to seke?[1]

This manifestly involves an utter abandonment of the attitude so long sustained, and
therein lies its irresistible appeal. The Troilus is
not milk for babes; but it is a great work of art,
and as such, I believe, inevitably ethical. It is
our own fault, not Chaucer's, if we miss the
application.

Yet, even after this parting, moving as it is,
and sincerely expressive of the poet's nature,

[1] v. 1828-1848.

Chaucer cannot say farewell without turning his irony upon himself.

> Lo here, of payens corsed olde rites,
> Lo here, what alle hire goddes may availle;
> Lo here, thise wrecched worldes appetites;
> Lo here, the fyn and guerdoun for travaille
> Of Jove, Appollo, of Mars, of swich rascaille!
> Lo here, the forme of olde clerkis speche
> In poetrie, if ye hire bokes seche.

Who am I, that I should exhort you to turn aside from the follies of love and the vanities of human endeavor? A mere student, poring over my ancient books and repeating, as so many have done before me, the wonderful and transitory things that they record; a versifier, humbly tracing the footsteps of Virgil, and Ovid, and Homer, and Lucan, and Statius: —

> Lo here, the forme of olde clerkis speche
> In poetrie, if ye hire bokes seche.

And so the Troilus closes, with a dedication to Strode and Gower and a prayer to the Triune God: —

> Thow oon, and two, and thre, eterne on lyve,
> That regnest ay in thre, and two, and oon,
> Uncircumscript, and al maist circumscrive,
> Us from visible and invisible foon
> Defende, and to thy mercy, everichon,
> So make us, Jesus, for thi mercy digne,
> For love of mayde and moder thyn benigne.

V

THE CANTERBURY TALES — I

THE Canterbury Tales exists in fragments, which no one has ever succeeded in fitting together. Different manuscripts arrange them in different ways, and modern scholars have exhibited much ingenuity in trying to make out the right order of the several stories. Of late, there has been a disposition amongst the learned to believe either that Chaucer made more than one tentative arrangement, or that he never settled the matter in his mind at all. These are questions, however, that need not now detain us. The plan is clear enough for our immediate purposes. We may profitably study the tales in groups, without regard to disputed problems of order.

We know, at least, that the series begins with the Knight, the Miller, the Reeve, and the Cook, and ends with the Manciple and the Parson. Within these extremities, we can make out several groups, each of which holds together. One of the longest of these begins with the Shipman's Prologue and ends with the Nun's Priest's Epilogue, containing the tales of the Shipman, the Prioress, Chaucer himself (namely, two, Sir Thopas and the Melibee), the Monk, and the Nun's Priest. This group is admirably organized. Another, still longer, which is called the Marriage Group, begins with the Wife of Bath's Prologue and ends with the Franklin's Tale: the order is Wife, Friar, Sumner, Clerk, Merchant, Squire, Franklin. The Physician's Tale and the Pardoner's also form a group; so do the Second Nun's and the Canon's Yeoman's. The Tale of the Man of Law stands, in a manner, by itself, with an elaborate introduction which makes it clear that it was to begin the day. By common consent it is placed after the Cook's fragment. It will not be possible, in the limited time at my disposal, to consider every group of tales. I shall make a selection, therefore, with a view to illustrate Chaucer's art in the two main points of character and dramatic method.

There has been a rather active discussion, for more than a hundred years, concerning the probable source of Chaucer's scheme of the Canterbury Pilgrimage. The result is a *non liquet*. Several possible models have been pointed out, and others are turning up continually. The *pros* and *cons* in every case have been argued with learning and ingenuity. So far as I can see, however, the advocates of each new source, though they have found it easy to demolish the arguments of their predecessors, have not been quite so successful in constructing acceptable theories of their own. There is, then, no single collection of tales to which we can point, with any confidence, as that which gave Chaucer the hint.

This condition of things should not surprise us. It is what we ought to expect, and the inference is easy. The plan of attaching stories together so as to make a collection is very old, very widespread, and very obvious. It was a traditional bit of technique, both in literature and in folklore, ages before Chaucer was born, and in all four quarters of the world. And furthermore, it was a bit of technique that accorded with actual practice. What could people do, in old times, but tell stories, when they were assembled and had plenty of leisure? The practice, indeed, has not died out, even in these days of novels and newspapers, and it was universal and inevitable, under all sorts of circumstances, when these time-killing but unsociable inventions did not yet exist. Chaucer's problem was not, to hunt through literature for an idea which confronted him, unsought, at every turn in life. That he knew collections of tales may be taken for granted; that he often followed convention is a matter of course. He had some knowledge of the literary device, and much knowledge of the immemorial habit of mankind.

That the particular frame which Chaucer adopted resembles this or that frame which preceded it in literary history, signifies nothing — except that some things in life are more or less like other things. Chaucer had no need to borrow or to invent: he needed only to observe. His genius appears, in the first place, in making a good choice among his several observations, in perceiving the advantages of one particular frame over all others. Pilgrims were as familiar sights to Chaucer as commercial travellers are to us. There is not one chance in a hundred that he had not gone on a Canterbury pilgrimage himself. And pilgrims did, for a fact, while away the time in story-telling. Newton did not learn that apples fall by reading treatises on pomology.

The most tantalizing of all the parallels, by the way, is Sercambi's *Novelle*, for which the frame is likewise a pilgrimage. But it is hard to get an historical point of contact. Dates are right enough, and geography does not interfere. It is even conceivable that Chaucer and Sercambi met in Italy, though there is no evidence either way. The difficulties are less tangible than dates and places; but, such as they are, they cannot be surmounted. Yet, after all, Sercambi's scheme is a precious document in the case, though not in proof of imitation. What it does show, is that it was possible for a writer of far less originality than Chaucer to hit upon the device of a pilgrimage as a convenient frame for a collection of stories.

Before the idea of a pilgrimage occurred to him, Chaucer had twice undertaken to compose a series of tales. The results lie before us in the Tragedies, afterwards assigned to the Monk, and the Legend of Cupid's Saints, otherwise known as Good Women. Both works exhibit, in the most striking fashion, the orderly habits of mediæval literature. They likewise prove, beyond cavil, the docility of Chaucer himself, the instinctive readiness with which he deferred to technical authority and bowed his neck to the rhetorical yoke. The lesson is salutary. We perceive, in this great poet, not a vast, irregular, untaught genius, — an amiable but terrible infant, impatient of regulation, acknowledging no laws of structure, guided by no canons of criticism. Quite the contrary! Chaucer was a conscientious student of literary form. He submitted with patient eagerness to the precepts of his teachers. Schematism was the governing principle of their instruction, and he had no wish to rebel. Thus he got the training which enabled him, when the time came, to give free rein to his vivacious originality without losing his self-control.

From these considerations there emerges a rule

of judgment that is of some value for our guidance in interpreting Chaucer's final masterpiece,
the Canterbury Tales. It may be stated in the
simplest language: *Chaucer always knew what he
was about.* When, therefore, he seems to be violat-
ing dramatic fitness, — as in the ironical tribute of
the Clerk to the Wife of Bath, or the monstrous
cynicism of the Pardoner's confessions, — we
must look to our steps. Headlong inferences are
dangerous. We are dealing with a great literary
artist who had been through the schools. The
chances are that such details are not casual
flourishes. Somehow, in all likelihood, they fall
into decorous subordination to his main design.

This design, as we know, is a pilgrimage to
Canterbury. I have spoken of it, for convenience,
as a "frame." That, indeed, is the light in which
it is commonly regarded. We read each tale by
itself, as if it were an isolated unit; often, indeed,
as if Chaucer were telling it in his own person.
At most, we inquire, in a half-hearted fashion,
whether it is appropriate to the character of the
Knight, or the Sumner, or the Franklin. Very
seldom do we venture to regard the several stories from the dramatic point of view. Yet that is
manifestly our paramount duty.

Many and great were the advantages that
Chaucer discerned in his plot of a Canterbury
pilgrimage. They stand out in sharp contrast

against the monotonous background of his two earlier experiments, the Tragedies and the Legend, to which we may return for a moment.

Each of these is unified not by structure but by subject matter. The unity, therefore, is not organic, but mechanical. In the Tragedies, — for the idea of which Chaucer was indebted in equal measure to the Romance of the Rose and Boccaccio's *De Casibus*, — we have a number of sombre sketches, rather declamatory than narrative, of exalted personages whom Fortune brought low. In the Good Women, — a singular cross between the *Legenda Aurea* and Ovid's *Heroides*, with a charming prologue, which reverts for its machinery to the French love-visions, — we read the lives of famous ladies of ancient days who suffered death, or worse, for love of faithless men. In both works the plan is absolutely rigid. Variety in form or matter is excluded by the convention adopted (tragedy, in the one; legend in the other) and by the limitations of the theme. Movement is impossible, for there is no connection between the parts. Dramatic presentation is not attempted, or even thought of, all the stories being told by one person, the poet himself.

Turn now to the Canterbury Tales, and the change is startling. It results, in the last analysis, from Chaucer's adopting the scheme of a Canterbury pilgrimage. The stories are no longer alike

in form or subject, nor are they all in one key.
There is infinite variety, because they are told by
a variety of persons. Every reader may discover
something to his taste, both in style and substance, as Chaucer himself protests in his apology for the Miller, "who tolde his cherles tale in
his manere." Those who do not fancy low comedy may find enough of polite history, as well as
of morality and religion.

> And therfore, whoso list it nat yheere,
> Turne over the leef and chese another tale;
> For he shal fynde ynowe, grete and smale,
> Of storial thyng that toucheth gentillesse,
> And eek moralitee and hoolynesse.
> Blameth nat me if that ye chese amys.

But this is not all. Chaucer's adoption of a
Canterbury pilgrimage was not a mere excuse for
story-telling. Most readers, I am aware, treat
this great masterpiece simply as a storehouse of
fiction, and so do many critics. Yet everybody
feels, I am sure, that Chaucer was quite as much
interested in the Pilgrims themselves as in their
several narratives. This, no doubt, is what Dryden had in mind when he wrote, comparing
Chaucer with Ovid: "Both of them understood
the manners, under which name I comprehend
the passions, and, in a larger sense, the descrip-
tions of persons, and their very habits. For an

[1] A. 3176–3181.

example, I see Baucis and Philemon as perfectly before me, as if some ancient painter had drawn them; and all the pilgrims in the Canterbury Tales, — their humors, their features, and the very dress, as distinctly as if I had supped with them at the Tabard in Southwark; yet even there too the figures in Chaucer are much more lively, and set in a better light."

I am much deceived if Dryden is not here treading on the verge of the proposition that the Canterbury Tales is, to all intents and purposes, a Human Comedy. Certainly he is calling our attention to something that distinguishes Chaucer's work from every collection of stories that preceded it. It was much, as we have seen, that Chaucer had the judgment, among the infinite doings of the world, to select a pilgrimage, and to parcel out his tales to the miscellaneous company that met at the Tabard on the way to Canterbury. It was more, far more, that he had the genius to create the Pilgrims, endowing each of them with an individuality that goes much beyond the typical. If we had only the Prologue, we might, perhaps, regard the Pilgrims as types. The error is common, and venial. But we must not stop with the Prologue: we must go on to the play. The Pilgrims are not static: they move and live. The Canterbury Pilgrimage is, whether Dryden meant it or not, a Human Comedy, and

the Knight and the Miller and the Pardoner and
the Wife of Bath and the rest are the *dramatis
personae.* The Prologue itself is not merely a
prologue: it is the first act, which sets the personages in motion. Thereafter, they move by
virtue of their inherent vitality, not as tale-tell-
ing puppets, but as men and women. From
this point of view, which surely accords with
Chaucer's intention, the Pilgrims do not exist
for the sake of the stories, but *vice versa.* Struc-
turally regarded, the stories are merely long
speeches expressing, directly or indirectly, the
characters of the several persons. They are more
or less comparable, in this regard, to the soliloquies of Hamlet or Iago or Macbeth. But they
are not mere monologues, for each is addressed
to all the other personages, and evokes reply and
comment, being thus, in a real sense, a part of
the conversation.

Further, — and this is a point of crucial significance, — the action of the plot, however simple,
involves a great variety of relations among the
Pilgrims. They are brought together by a common impulse, into a casual and impermanent
association, which is nevertheless, for the time
being, peculiarly intimate. They move slowly
along the road, from village to village and inn to
inn, in groups that are ever shifting, but ever
forming afresh. Things happen to them. They

come to know each other better and better.
Their personalities act and react. Friendships
combine for the nonce. Jokes are cracked, like
the Host's on the Pardoner, which are taken
amiss. Smouldering enmities of class or profession, like that between the Sumner and the Friar,
which was proverbial, blaze into flaming quar-
rels. Thus the story of any pilgrim may be affected or determined, — in its contents, or in the
manner of the telling, or in both, — not only by
his character in general, but also by the circumstances, by the situation, by his momentary relations to the others in the company, or even by
something in a tale that has come before. We
lose much, therefore, when we neglect the so-
called prologues and epilogues, and the bits of
conversation and narrative that link the tales
together. Many more of these would have been
supplied if Chaucer had not left his work in so
fragmentary a condition; but such as we have
are invaluable, both for their own excellence, and
for the light they throw upon the scope and
details of the great design.

Chaucer's contemporaries were quite aware
of the dramatic nature of the Pilgrimage and the
significance of the Pilgrims as characters in the
comedy. Their appreciation is put beyond a
peradventure by that highly interesting document, the Tale of Beryn, — written not long

after Chaucer's death by an anonymous versifier for insertion in the Canterbury scheme.
The Beryn itself, which is assigned to the Merchant as the first story on the return journey,
need not detain us. The prologue, however, is
worth a moment's notice.

This describes the arrival of the party at
the Checker inn at Canterbury, and their proceedings, grave and gay, until they set out for
London. Much space is given to the adventures
of the Pardoner with a tapster, which result in
his losing some money and getting his head
broken. The scene in the cathedral is more edifying, and equally vivid. Particularly diverting
is the behavior of the Miller and others of his
sort. While the Knight and his compeers go
straightway to the shrine of Saint Thomas to
pray and make offering, these idle fellows stroll
about the church, staring at the stained-glass
windows, misinterpreting the scenes therein de-
picted, and pretending, like gentlemen, to
blazon the coats of arms. The Host calls them
to order and directs them to the martyr's tomb.
By-and-by the company scatter, to see the
sights of the town or to call upon their friends,
while the Wife of Bath and the Prioress walk
about the inn garden. They reassemble for supper, at which the Host acts as marshal.

All this is a poor substitute for what Chaucer

would have given us, if he had lived to finish
his work. But there is some merit in the performance, and it certainly evinces a lively sense
of the actuality of Chaucer's Pilgrims. The
author of Beryn did not mistake the Canterbury Tales for a volume of disconnected stories.
He recognized the work for what it really is —
a micro-cosmography, a little image of the great
world.

Travel, as everybody knows, is for the time
being a mighty leveller of social distinctions,
particularly when its concomitants throw the
voyagers together while at the same time iso-
lating them from the rest of the world. Think
of the smoking-room of a small steamship with
only three or four dozen passengers. These men
might live side by side in one row of brick houses
for a hundred years and scarcely know each
other's faces. Break the shaft, keep them at sea
for an extra week, and, if they are n't careful and
if the cigars hold out, they will empty their
hearts to one another with an indiscretion that
may shock them to death when they remember
it ashore.

Now an organized company of Pilgrims — and
Chaucer's Pilgrims had effected an organization
at Harry Bailly's inn — were brought together
in a similar intimacy, which was made especially
close by the religious impulse that actuated them

all in common. We must not be skeptical about
the genuineness of this impulse, merely because
some of the Pilgrims are loose fish, or because
they do not always act and speak with propriety.
If we let this consideration much affect us, it
must be either because we are uninstructed in
mediæval manners, or because we apply our
own religion to life in a deplorably wooden
fashion. This score and a half of miscellaneous
Englishmen and Englishwomen were fulfilling
the vow they had made to St. Thomas in sickness or danger or misfortune. However diverse
their stations in life, their moral codes, or the sincerity of their religion in general, — and in all
these points there is variety so rich as almost to
bewilder, — here they were at one. The saint
had helped them, and they were gratefully doing
their duty in return.

But the occasion was not only religious, it
was social. Listen to the Host, who has entertained hundreds of such companies at the
Tabard Inn: —

> Ye goon to Caunterbury — God yow speede,
> The blisful martir quite yow youre meede!
> And wel I woot, as ye goon by the weye,
> *Ye shapen yow to talen and to pleye;*
> For trewely, confort ne myrthe is noon
> To ride by the weye doumb as a stoon.

The occasion, then, was both religious and
social; and the various Pilgrims, knowing that

all men are equal in God's sight, were not indisposed to sink their differences of rank for the nonce, so far, at least, as to laugh and talk together without the stand-offish punctilio of rigid etiquette.

Chaucer's own birth and station, as I reminded you in my opening lecture, had brought him into easy contact with both high and low; and his experiences as burgher, soldier, courtier, officeholder, and diplomatic agent had given him unparalleled opportunities for observation, which his humorously sympathetic temperament had impelled him to use to the best advantage. Mankind was his specialty. He was now a trained and practised writer, with a profound sense of the joy and beauty, the sadness and irony, of human life. He had already studied the whole world from the point of view of two of the ruling passions: — the desire for reputation (in the House of Fame) and passionate love (in the Troilus). In both of these great works, however, his approach had been, so to speak, oblique or indirect: by symbolism or allegory in the one; in the other, by way of a return to the days of old. Now, at length, in this Canterbury Pilgrimage, with its nine-and-twenty contemporary human creatures, he has recognized his crowning opportunity. He will show life as it is; he will paint "what he sees"! But I am wrong. It is not showing (or exhibition); it is not painting (or delineation): it is dramatic action. And so he makes himself one of the Pilgrims, in order that we may understand that they are as real as he is. Chaucer existed, thus we instinctively syllogize, and therefore the Prioress existed, and the Reeve, and the Manciple, and the Monk, and the Knight, and Harry Bailly, the incomparable innkeeper, to whom, and not to Geoffrey Chaucer, the conduct of the drama is entrusted. Chaucer reports, but Harry Bailly is the dynamic agent. The action of the piece is largely due to his initiative, and to him are referable the details again and again. Sometimes, to be sure, the play gets out of hand, but not for long; and usually, on such occasions, he is content to let go the reins, since the team is guiding itself.

The Host, as we know, is the appointed leader. He nominates himself for the office, as many a good politician has done before and since, but not until after supper, when his social qualities have been fully tested. He is well fitted for the office — a fine large man, handsome after his florid fashion, merry, afraid of nobody — "of manhood him lakkede right nought" — loud-voiced and free-spoken. It is not by accident that Chaucer calls him as fair a burgess as there is in Cheap; for London was an *imperium in imperio*, and the citizens were persons of importance, not merely in their own eyes, but in the estimation of all orders and even of the king. Chaucer himself, who was always in politics, — would that we had his political autobiography!— is a first-rate example of a "king's man," a sort of courtier who was also a burgher by descent and in actuality. Once a Londoner, always a Londoner, no matter what else you might become.

But Harry Bailly was not only a fair and seemly burgess, bold of his speech. He was "wys and wel ytaught": that is, in modern parlance, a discreet man, with plenty of tact, one who "knew his way about"; he had some education and was thoroughly versed in the usages of society. His hearty and sometimes boisterous manner must not deceive us. It is partly temperament, partly professional technique, and he forces it a little now and then, for a very special purpose — to see if he cannot irritate some pilgrim or other into revolt; for whoever gainsays his judgment must pay an enormous forfeit, no less than the total travelling expenses of the company.

"and whoso wole my juggement withseye
  Shal paye al that we spenden by the weye."

Harry is the legitimate ancestor of many a jovial and autocratic innkeeper in our literature; but

we must not confuse him with such roaring eccen-
trics as Blague the landlord of the George at
Waltham in the Merry Devil of Edmonton, or
even mine Host of the Garter in the Merry
Wives. "Ha!" cries Blague, "I'll caper in my
own fee simple. Away with punctilios and orthog-
raphy! I serve the good Duke of Norfolk.
Bilbo! *Tityre tu patulae recubans sub tegmine
fagi.*" Blague, it appears, is "well ytaught," for
he can quote Virgil, with a prophecy, one is
tempted to conjecture, of the *Tityre-tu's* of the
next generation; but after all he is only a kind of
substantial and well-esteemed buffoon. He is
not Harry Bailly — scarcely more so than Sir
John Falstaff (rest his soul!) is Chaucer's Knight.
For Harry has his own dignity: he knows the
times and the manners. Here, as ever, Chaucer
is quite specific. The landlord of the Tabard, so
he tells us, was

> a semely man ... withalle
> For to han been a marchal in an halle.

Such as he had been master of ceremonies many
a time when our Knight had "begun the board,"
or sat at the head of the table, at high chivalric
festivals.

Yet, despite the Host's autocracy, the ruler of
the company is actually the Knight. It is he that
asserts himself whenever the case requires an
appeal to the controlling forces of the social

world. One of these crises arrives when the Monk gets halfway — a quarter, who can tell? — through his list of tragedies, or tales of men and women fallen from their high estate. The Monk belonged to the "gentles," and the Host was not so ready to interrupt him as in the case of Chaucer, who was a somewhat ambiguous personality, even to the omniscient Bailly. Not altogether because Harry was considerate. He stood in no awe of Dan Piers; the preliminaries demonstrate that. He was simply at his wit's end. This roll of dismal biographies must close sometime; but it is like many a sermon: at every pause, one thinks the peroration has passed, only to discover that the preacher has got his second wind, or his thirteenth; and one feels a certain reluctance to imitate the historic Scotswoman and throw a footstool at the parson's head! Besides, Harry Bailly was well taught, and he was rather a Saxon than a Celt. He did agnize a natural and prompt alacrity he felt in boredom. It is all very well to be entertained; but now then there is a time for edification, and anything that's stupid must be edifying. In my part of the country we call this the New England conscience. Hence Harry was hesitant. "Lucifer, Adam, Zenobia, Crœsus, Pedro of Spain, Bernabò Visconti," — these be good words! *Rusticus exspectat!* Patience! the river will flow by if we wait a bit. In short, Harry was "out of his epoch"; the situation was just a trifle beyond his control; and so the natural leader asserted himself, as many a time on the perilous edge of battle when it raged.

Chaucer, they tell us, is very modern. So he is; this crisis proves it. You can translate his situations into our own at any given moment. Darken the theatre for a second — then turn up the lights. Vanishes the road to Canterbury; vanish the Pilgrims on their way to St. Thomas's shrine. Appear, at table, a party of gentlemen; a helpless toastmaster, twirling his eyeglasses and stealing glances at his watch. Time flies, death urges — and there are several speakers left on the list which he has scribbled off upon his cuff. And here, — intrenched, unassailable, standing like Teneriffe, — is the lord of the ascendant, the after-dinner platitudinarian, droning on and on, his ten minutes elongated by imperceptible gradations to five-and-twenty, and still no sign that he is nearing the seamark of his utmost sail! And this is precisely the address that will be reported at greatest length in the morrow's newspaper, and that a grateful constituency will hold it a precious privilege to read.

Nowadays there is no help for it; but they did things better in the fourteenth century. There

was the Knight! He had been at Alexandria
when it was won; he had fought for our faith in
Tremezen; he had seen service with pagan
against pagan, with the lord of Palathia against
another heathen in Turkey.

"Hoo!" quod the Knyght, "good sire, namoore of this!
That ye han seyd is right ynough, ywis,
And muchel moore; for litel hevynesse
Is right ynough to muche folk, I gesse."

The toastmaster rallies; Harry Bailly is himself
again: —

"Sire Monk, namoore of this, so God yow blesse!
Youre tale anoyeth al this compaignye.
Swich talkyng is nat worth a boterflye,
For therinne is ther no desport ne game."

This is the first instance in which the Knight
saves the situation. There are but two. The second is even more critical. For the toastmaster
has lost his self-control. This is the famous incident of the quarrel between the Pardoner
and the Host, a comic interlude with a tragedy
behind it, to which we shall return.

In earlier works, we have seen Chaucer yielding with docility to mediæval schematism. But
now, in the Canterbury Tales, by setting his
Pilgrimage in motion, he breaks definitively with
all such rigid notions of order. The Knight, to
be sure, begins the series of tales, by the com-
plaisance of the lots, Fortune showing herself

deferential to rank and dignity. But this is the poet's valediction to the old-fashioned method. Henceforth, it is dramatic considerations that must govern order: tabular views give way to human life in action.

With drastic realism, the boldness of which we can hardly appreciate in these days of unconventionality, the drunken Miller thrusts himself forward to tell a story as soon as the Knight has finished his romance of Palamon and Arcite. "He knows a noble tale," he vociferates, "which will fitly recompense the chevalier."

Harry Bailly had intended a more decorous procedure. He has already called upon the Monk, an important personage, to follow the Knight, and he expostulates with the Miller, begging him to give way to "some better man," that is, some one of higher station. But the Miller has a drunken man's obstinacy, and the Host assents, rather than break up the entertainment with a vulgar quarrel. The Reeve takes the Miller's Tale as a personal insult, and wishes to answer it. Hereafter, there is no returning to any artificial scheme.

Two acts in Chaucer's Human Comedy are so completely wrought that we may study their dramatic structure with confidence. One of these is the group of tales beginning with the Wife of Bath's Prologue and ending with the story of the

Franklin, of which I shall speak with some fulness in my next lecture. The other is the group that begins with the Shipman's Prologue and includes (besides the fabliau of that famous master mariner) the Prioress's Tale, Sir Thopas, the Melibee, the Monk's dismal Tragedies, and the Nun's Priest's masterpiece of the Cock and Fox.

For some reason the Host thinks that time is ripe for a serious discourse, and so he calls upon the Parson; but in so doing he is guilty of an infraction of the rules of good taste: he swears like a pirate.

> "Sir Parisshe Prest," quod he, "for Goddes bones,
> Telle us a tale, as was thi forward yore.
> I se wel that ye lerned men in lore
> Can moche good, by Goddes dignitee!"

The Parson is accustomed to reprove sinners — "to snub them sharply," the Prologue tells us, "whenever the occasion seems to call for it" — and he is not remiss now:

> The Parson hem answerde, "*Benedicite*!
> What eyleth the man, so synfully to swere?"

This evokes a jocose reply from Harry Bailly, in which he accuses the good priest of being a Lollard, and bids the company lend their ears to the impending sermon.

> Oure Host answerde, "O Jankin, be ye there?
> I smelle a Lollere in the wynd," quod he.

"Now! goode men," quod oure Hoste, "herkeneth me;
Abydeth, for Goddes digne passioun,
For we schal han a predicacioun;
This Lollere heer wil prechen us somwhat!"

"Not a bit of it!" cries the Shipman. "We'll
have no heretical preaching here! This priest
wishes to sow tares among the clean wheat of
our orthodoxy. I will block his game by telling
a story myself." Let us not misunderstand the
Captain. It is not Lollardry that he is in a panic
about, but a sermon. He is eager for mirth, and
desperately afraid of being bored.

The Host, we remember, is the absolute ruler
of the company with respect to the order of
stories. There is a very large forfeit hanging
over any pilgrim who rebels against his judgment, no less than the total of the travelling
expenses. To this the Pilgrims have not only
assented by unanimous vote, but they have
confirmed their suffrages by a solemn oath, after
the true mediæval manner.

Technically, no doubt, the Shipman's out-
break might be taken as insubordination. In
spirit, however, there is no revolt; and Harry
gives a tacit approval, in the interest of variety:
for it is well, after all, that the serious narrative
of a "learned man in lore" should be followed
by something humorous, and that is what the
mariner promises.

"And therfore, Hoost, I warne thee biforn,
My joly body schal a tale telle,
And I schal clynken you so mery a belle,
That I schal waken al this compaignie."

Perhaps there had been a tendency to somno-
lence in the "thrifty tale" that had gone before.
Certainly there was such a tendency if, as some
think, it was the Melibee, which is largely occupied with the pitilessly long-winded arguments of the good wife Prudence. At all events,
the Shipman keeps his word. Nobody went to
sleep, I am sure, while he was talking. And the
Merchant, the Monk, and the Wife of Bath
must have paid him very particular attention.

The Shipman's Tale was originally intended
for a woman; for the Wife of Bath, beyond a
doubt. It accords with her character both in
style and in sentiment. Its tone is hers precisely,
frankly sensual, — unmoral, if you like, — but
too hearty and too profoundly normal to be un-
wholesome. And there are many expressions in
the story which were clearly written for her and
for her alone.

The tale turns upon a trick by which a rich
merchant was cheated out of a sum of money
by Dan John, a monk, with certain incidental
deceptions which we may ignore. The Wife of
Bath knew many merchants. As a maker of
cloth, she had, quite possibly, recollections not

altogether pleasant of her dealings with such personages, though we may feel pretty confident that they had seldom got ahead of her in a bargain. But Chaucer changed his plan, and it is vastly interesting to see his masterpiece gradually taking shape as he goes on with it. Even as he wrote the tale of Dan John and the merchant, the Wife of Bath's character grew upon him. He conceived the happy idea of devoting a whole act of his Human Comedy to the discussion of Marriage, and he saw that nobody could be so well fitted as the Wife to precipitate such a discussion, and to control it while it lasted. With this in view, he furnished her with a succession of five husbands, and with a monstrously heretical tenet as to the Subjection of Men. This development of his plan released the story of Dan John and the merchant, and Chaucer assigned it to the Shipman, to whom it was almost as appropriate. For our master mariner was engaged in the foreign trade, and had no objection to satirizing the merchants who chartered his barge, the Maudlin. Indeed, he used to take large toll from the cargo, when that consisted of wine: —

> Ful many a draughte of wyn had he ydrawe
> Fro Burdeux-ward, whil that the chapman sleep.
> Of nyce conscience took he no keep.

Of course, the presence of a substantial and very

dignified merchant among the Pilgrims gave special zest, for both Wife and Shipman, to the telling of this particular tale.

Here we have again a trait of Chaucer's method, or, let us rather say, another proof of his fruitful observation of life. An anecdote always gains point if there is somebody present whom it may be thought to hit. Again and again is this principle expressly recognized by the Canterbury Pilgrims. The Miller's Tale concerns a carpenter, and the Reeve, who is of that trade, suspects that it is aimed at him: —

> "This dronke Millere hath ytoold us heer
> How that bigyled was a carpenteer,
> Peraventure in scorn, for I am oon.
> And, by youre leve, I shal hym quite anoon."

And so the saturnine Oswald returns the compliment in a tale of a miller. The Cook's Tale, fortunately a fragment, was to be of an innkeeper, and was avowedly a reply to the Host's attack upon the artifices of chefs and caterers. The Friar and the Sumner furnish a similar comic interlude at each other's expense. All these are obvious and familiar instances; but what is expressly stated in these cases, we are left to extend, when we see occasion, to other tales, as well as to the conversation of the Pilgrims. And this story of the Shipman's is a case in point. Indications are abundant, as any one may see for himself by comparing the character of the Merchant in the general prologue with the words and demeanor of the merchant in the Shipman's Tale. One passage is enough for my purpose. Says the Shipman's merchant:

> "Wyf," quod this man, "litel kanstow devyne
> The curious bisynesse that we have.
> For of us chapmen, also God me save,
> And by that lord that clepid is Seint Yve,
> Scarsly amonges twelve tweye shul thryve
> Continuelly, lastynge unto oure age.
> We may wel make chiere and good visage.
> And dryve forth the world as it may be,
> And kepen oure estaat in pryvetee,
> Til we be deed, or elles that we pleye
> A pilgrymage, or goon out of the weye.
> And therfore have I greet necessitee
> Upon this queynte world t'avyse me;
> For everemoore we moote stonde in drede
> Of hap and fortune in oure chapmanhede."

When this was uttered, did not every man and woman in the company look at the Merchant? "Perhaps," they thought, "he too is playing a pilgrimage to dodge his creditors." But they could not believe such a thing.

> Ther wiste no wight that he was in dette,
> So estatly was he of his governaunce.

Chaucer does not know that he is in debt either. He merely suggests it as a possibility, as something incident to a merchant's life.

Now the Shipman's Tale is not merely a jest at

the expense of merchants. It touches up the monks as well. Dan John was, in rank and station, just such a man as the Monk of the Pilgrimage. Both were persons of position in their order, often entrusted with important business by their abbot. Chaucer's Monk is expressly called an "out-rider," and the Shipman's Dan John received a commission from his superior to "ride out" — that is, to make a tour of inspection in regard to the remoter farms and rented properties of the monastery. The Host receives the story with loud acclaim, and exhorts the company to heed the moral: — "Aha, fellows! be on your guard against such tricks. Don't invite any monks to visit your houses." Naturally, he points his remarks by a look or a gesture, so as to raise a laugh at the stately Monk who is riding among the Pilgrims on his berry-brown palfrey, with bridle jingling as loud and clear as the chapel-bell. And later, when he calls on him for a story in his turn, he alludes with sufficient definiteness to the Shipman's fabliau, even asking him if his name is not likewise Dan John. The Prioress is listening, and when, in her tale of the murdered little boy, she has occasion to mention an abbot who was true to his sacred office and had the grace of God to work a miracle, she cannot ignore the Host's gibe. "This abbot," says the Prioress, —

"This abbot, which that was an hooly man,
  As monkes been — or elles oghte be."

And again: "This holy man, this abbot, him
mene I." This is not satire; it is a tribute, rather,
which may serve to correct the Host for his flip-
pancy without being precisely a rebuke. There
may be bad monks in the world; but the Prioress
has no personal knowledge of any such, and is
not disposed to lend an ear to current slander.

Of all the Canterbury Pilgrims none is more
sympathetically conceived or more delicately
portrayed than Madame Eglantine, the prioress.
The impression she has made upon the company is exquisitely suggested by the courtesy
with which the Host invites her to tell a story
after the Shipman has finished. His softness of
speech and manner contrasts strongly with the
robust badinage that immediately precedes.

"Wel seyd, by *corpus dominus*," quod oure Hoost,
"Now longe moote thou saille by the cost,
  Sire gentil maister, gentil maryneer!
  God yeve the monk a thousand last quade yeer!
  A ha! felawes! beth ware of swich a jape!
  The monk putte in the mannes hood an ape,
  And in his wyves eek, by Seint Austyn!
  Draweth no monkes moore unto youre in.
  But now passe over, and lat us seke aboute,
Who shal now telle first of al this route
  Another tale;" and with that word he sayde,
  As curteisly as it had been a mayde,
"My lady Prioresse, by youre leve,

So that I wiste I sholde yow nat greve,
I wolde demen that ye tellen sholde
A tale next, if so were that ye wolde.
Now wol ye vouche sauf, my lady deere?"
   "Gladly," quod she, and seyde as ye shal heere.

The Prioress is of noble blood, and has been brought up from youth in a religious order; but it is a rich order, of the kind to which parents of wealth and position entrusted, as they still entrust, their daughters for care and education. She travels in modest state, with a nun for her secretary, and three attendant priests, who suffice on occasion to guard her from unpleasant contact with the rougher elements in the company. But her gentleness and sweet dignity are her best protection. She lives, as it were, in a cloister, even on the road to Canterbury. Yet she does not hold herself aloof. She is fond of society and shows no stiffness of demeanor. Her conversational talents are particularly insisted on. She is excellent company — "of greet desport" — and very pleasant and amiable in her demeanor.

And peyned hire to countrefete cheere
Of court, and to been estatlich of manere.

This couplet is often sadly misunderstood, as if the Prioress's bearing were a labored and affected imitation of polite behavior. It implies merely that her manners were exquisitely courtly, with that little touch of preciseness and finish which shows that one regards such things as of some concern. Her position in life required this of her, and it accorded with her nature as well. As to her table manners, which often make the uninstructed laugh, they are simply the perfection of mediæval daintiness. Nothing is farther from Chaucer's thought than to poke fun at them. Her greatest oath (for in those days everybody swore) was "by St. Loy." Could there be a sweeter or more ladylike expletive? It is soft and liquid, and above all, it does not distort the lips. Her little dogs went with her on the journey, and she watched over them with anxious affection: —

> But soore wepte she if oon of hem were deed,
> Or if men smoot it with a yerde smerte.

It is no accident that Chaucer makes her tell the infinitely pathetic legend of the pious little boy who was murdered for his childlike devotion to the Blessed Virgin. "This little child," she calls him, "learning his little book, as he sat in the school at his primer."

> This litel child, his litel book lernynge,
> As he sat in the scole at his prymer,
> He *Alma redemptoris* herde synge,
> As children lerned hire antiphoner;
> And as he dorste, he drough hym ner and ner,
> And herkned ay the wordes and the noote,
> Til he the firste vers koude al by rote.

Noght wiste he what this Latyn was to seye,
For he so yong and tendre was of age.
But on a day his felawe gan he preye
T'expounden hym this song in his langage,
Or telle hym why this song was in usage;
This preyde he hym to construe and declare
Ful often tyme upon his knowes bare.

His felawe, which that elder was than he,
Answerde hym thus: "This song, I have herd seye,
Was maked of our blisful Lady free,
Hire to salue, and eek hire for to preye
To been oure help and socour whan we deye.
I kan namoore expounde in this mateere;
I lerne song, I kan but smal grammeere."

　"And is this song maked in reverence
Of Cristes mooder?" seyde this innocent.
"Now, certes, I wol do my diligence
To konne it al er Cristemasse be went.
Though that I for my prymer shal be shent,
And shal be beten thries in an houre,
I wol it konne Oure Lady for to honoure!"

His mother looked for him at night, but he did
not come home, and she sought him everywhere
— "with modres pitee in her brest enclosed."
What can the Prioress know of a mother's feelings? Everything, though she is never to have
children, having chosen, so she thought, the better part. But her heart goes out, in yearnings
which she does not comprehend or try to analyze,
to little dogs, and little boys at school. Nowhere
is the poignant trait of thwarted motherhood so
affecting as in this character of the Prioress.

You do not care to hear from me that Geoffrey Chaucer took pleasure in birds and flowers and running brooks, that he loved the sunshine on the grass or as it streamed through storied windows, that it was a delight to him to walk in the dewy rides of the king's forest and see buck and doe and fawn in the distance, or watch the squirrels scamper up the beeches and spring from branch to branch and sit looking at him with their little beady eyes —

> And many sqwirelles, that sete
> Ful high upon the trees and ete,
> And in hir maner made festes.

Nor do you care to hear of his worship of "these flowers white and red, such as men callen daisies in our town."

These things are amiable and charming, but they are matters of every day. The supreme genius knows how to seize the moment of intensest self-revelation for each of his characters; and then, a phrase will do the business. It may be Menelaus to Helen, in Euripides: — "Leave you in Egypt! It was for you that I sacked Troy." Or Falstaff, musing as he grows old: — "O, it is much that a lie with a slight oath, and a jest with a sad brow, will do with a fellow that never had the ache in his shoulders." Or Lady Macbeth: — "Here's the smell o' the blood still. All the perfumes of Arabia will not sweeten this

little hand." And so in Chaucer — there is the
Wife of Bath, hugging to her tough old heart the
remembrance of her "world" that she has had
"in her time." There is Cressida, false to the
matchless Troilus, but promising herself to be
faithful to her new lover — "To Diomede algate I wol be trewe"; and the Pardoner, the
one lost soul among the Canterbury Pilgrims:
"Christ grant you his pardon! I will not deceive
you. God knows it is better than mine"; and
Madame Eglantine the holy nun, with her pious
legend of the little boy learning his little book.

VI

THE CANTERBURY TALES — II

MIRACLES of the Blessed Virgin were a favorite form of legend in the middle ages, and no wonder! Every student will recall, at the mere word, a score of these stories, delicately beautiful and of a pathos almost beyond belief. The Prioress, involuntarily expressive of her inmost nature, had chosen to repeat the loveliest and most touching of them all. Its effect upon the Pilgrims is described by Chaucer in two lines of utter simplicity, which touch, so I think, the skirts of Shakspere's garment: — "Whan seyd was this miracle, every man" — think what that means: the jangling Miller, the trumpet-voiced Sumner, the cynical and accursed Pardoner, the irrepressible Wife of Bath, the merry Friar, the Merchant, angry to the death under his mask of sedate respectability —

> Whan seyd was al this miracle, every man
> As sobre was that wonder was to se.

Nobody can command his thoughts or trust his voice. The whole troop is silent, till at last the Host, to relieve the tension, falls a-jesting, for it must be either laughter or tears; and the butt of

his humor is Geoffrey Chaucer, who is some-
where in the background, riding along in apparent abstraction with downcast eyes.

> Whan seyd was al this miracle, every man
> As sobre was that wonder was to se,
> Til that oure Hooste japen tho bigan,
> And thanne at erst he looked upon me,
> And seyde thus, "What man artow?" quod he;
> "Thou lookest as thou woldest fynde an hare,
> For evere upon the ground I se thee stare.
>
> "Approche neer, and looke up murily.
> Now war yow, sires, and lat this man have place!
> He in the waast is shape as wel as I;
> This were a popet in an arm t'enbrace
> For any womman, smal and fair of face.
> He semeth elvyssh by his contenaunce,
> For unto no wight dooth he daliaunce.
>
> "Sey now somwhat, syn oother folk han sayd;
> Telle us a tale of myrthe, and that anon."
> "Hooste," quod I, "ne beth nat yvele apayd,
> For oother tale certes kan I noon,
> But of a rym I lerned longe agoon."
> "Ye, that is good," quod he; "now shul we heere
> Som deyntee thyng, me thynketh by his cheere."

One thing is certain: we should not read this outburst of raillery without an attempt to visualize
the scene and imagine the action.

The Prioress's legend is received in silence;
there is a hush throughout the company. The
Host wishes to discharge the emotional forces,
and he picks out a quiet-looking Pilgrim as the

medium. The effect will be the greater, of course, if some demure person is called on for a tale of mirth. "And than at erste he looked upon me!" Not that this was the first time that Harry had seen Chaucer, but that he had not previously taken any notice of him. Chaucer rides forward at the summons, and is put on exhibition. The others make room for him, and the Host comments merrily upon his fulness of figure. Chaucer, then, has been effacing himself, riding with his eyes lowered, and making little or no conversation.

"He semeth elvyssh by his contenaunce,
    For unto no wight doth he daliaunce."

Contenaunce means not "visage" but "manner," and the aptest modern equivalent for *elvish* is "shy."

Are we to infer that Chaucer was, in real life, a diffident and uncompanionable person? Was he, like Addison, a man of no conversation, — "without a guinea in his pocket, though he could draw for a thousand pounds?" Possibly, but, in that case, what are we to make of the statement in the Prologue? "Once, when I had put up at the Tabard and was about to proceed on a pilgrimage to Canterbury, there arrived a company of nine-and-twenty persons; by sunset I had spoken with them every one, and was instantly admitted of their fellowship."

And shortly, whan the sonne was to reste,
So hadde I spoken with hem everichon
That I was of hir felaweshipe anon.

Here there is no chance for a double meaning or
any ironical jocosity. Chaucer was a guest at the
Tabard when the Pilgrims arrived, and he at
once made himself so agreeable that they in-
vited him to join the party. He circulated
among them, and actually spoke to every one
of the nine-and-twenty. This, beyond question,
is the real Chaucer. His quiet and abstracted
manner on the road is for the nonce; he is keeping
in the background, not because he is by temperament averse to sociability, but because he wishes
to play the part of a listener. He has undertaken,
in his own mind, the duty of reporting the pilgrimage, of rehearsing word for word every tale
that shall be told. That is why he effaces himself; and he rides with downcast eyes and ab-
stains from casual conversation, merely that he
may miss nothing of what is said. His staring
upon the ground does not prevent him from
noting every minutest detail of speech and
action. Let us banish, then, to the limbo of
fatuous ideas, the notion that Chaucer was shy,
along with the notion that he was naïf.

We know, at all events, that Chaucer was an
ironist, and never more so than at this very
moment; for he informs the Host that he does n't

remember any tale except an old rhyme about Sir Thopas, and when Harry stops this doggerel in full career, he begs to be informed, with an injured air, why he alone should thus be interfered with, since he is doing his very best!

"Why so?" quod I, "why wiltow lette me
Moore of my tale than another man,
Syn that it is the beste rym I kan?"

And he then proceeds to tell the Melibee, which all men have agreed is prosy enough. The next tale is the Monk's, and then comes the mock-heroic narrative of the Nun's Priest. Both of these we have already considered.

One other act of Chaucer's Human Comedy is complete (but for the story of Cambuscan) and highly finished. It begins with the Wife of Bath's Prologue and ends with the Tale of the Franklin. The subject is Marriage, which is discussed from several points of view, as the most important problem in organized society. The solution of the problem brings the act to an end.

The dominant figure in this act of the Comedy is the Wife of Bath. It is she who starts the debate, and the participants keep her steadily in mind, and mention her and her doctrines more than once. Even the comic interlude which breaks into the discussion is occasioned by her prologue. Nowhere is the dramatic spirit of the Canterbury Pilgrimage more evident than in this Marriage group of tales. Nowhere is it more important to heed the relations of the Pilgrims to each other. Neglect of this precaution has led to a good deal of misunderstanding.

The Wife's ostensible subject is Tribulation in Marriage. On this, she avers, she can speak with the authority of an expert, for she has outlived five husbands, worthy men in their degree, and she is ready to welcome a sixth when God shall send him.

> "Yblessed be God that I have wedded fyve!
> Welcome the sixte, whan that evere he shal."

Somebody — was it one of the clerics in the party? — has told her lately that she should have married but once. This dictum rankles: she finds no warrant for it in Scripture, and certainly none in her inclinations. Accordingly, she breaks forth in a vehement defence of her own principles and practices. The celibate life, she admits, may be a high and holy thing, well fitted for the Apostle Paul and other saints. Out of deference to them, she accords it the palm, for form's sake; but, at the same time, she makes her own position perfectly clear. She despises the ideal of the Church in this regard, and looks down with contempt upon all who aspire to it. Human nature is good enough for her. This is her first heresy; but she is so jovial in proclaiming it that no one takes offence, however strongly some of the Pilgrims may reprobate her principles in their hearts.

The Pardoner interrupts, in high glee. The dame has handled her scriptural texts with such skill, and set forth her doctrine so eloquently, that he cannot withhold his tribute of praise. "Ye been a noble prechour!" he protests, "but what you say is certainly enough to scare a man away from marriage." The compliment is not without significance, for the Pardoner is a good judge of preaching, being "a noble ecclesiaste" himself.

The Wife replies with great good humor, jocosely threatening further revelations.

> "Abyde!" quod she, "my tale is nat bigonne.
> Nay, thou shalt drynken of another tonne,
> Er that I go, shal savoure wors than ale.
> And whan that I have toold thee forth my tale
> Of tribulacion in mariage,
> Of which I am expert in al myn age,
> This is to seyn, myself have been the whippe, —
> Than maystow chese wheither thou wolt sippe
> Of thilke tonne that I shal abroche.
> Be war of it, er thou to ny approche;
> For I shal telle ensamples mo than ten."

The Pardoner urges her to continue. "Tell us young men," he begs, "some of your practical precepts." She consents, nothing loth, requesting the company, however, to take her jokes in good part.

The Wife proceeds, with infinite zest, to give
the history of her married life, unfolding, as she
does so, another heretical doctrine of a startling
kind, which, in fact, is the real subject of her discourse. This is nothing less than the dogma that
the wife is the head of the house. Obedience
is not her duty, but the husband's. Men are no
match for women, anyway. Let them sink back
to their proper level, and cease their ridiculous
efforts to maintain a position for which they
are not fit. Then marriages will all be happy.
Otherwise there is no hope for anything but
misery in wedlock. She supports her contention
with much curious learning, derived, of course,
from her fifth and latest husband, who was a
professional scholar; and she overbears opposition
by quoting her own experience, which is better
testimony than the citation of authorities. She
had always had her own way. Sometimes she
cowed her husbands, and sometimes she cajoled
them; but none of the five could resist her government. And it was well for them to yield.
This is happy marriage. Who should know so
well as she? Once, indeed, she rises almost to
sublimity, as she looks back on the joy of her
life:

"But, Lord Crist! whan that it remembreth me
Upon my yowthe, and on my jolitee,
It tikleth me aboute myn herte roote.

Unto this day it dooth myn herte boote
That I have had my world as in my tyme."[1]

This is one of the great dramatic utterances of human nature, as the Wife of Bath is one of the most amazing characters that the brain of man has ever yet conceived.

The Pilgrims, we may be sure, are not inattentive to the Wife's harangue. To the Prioress, her complete antithesis, it means little, either good or bad. She does not understand the language of the worldly widow. The Parson and the Clerk of course are scandalized: such heresies cannot pass unchallenged, even as a jest. Of the two, the Clerk has the greater cause for resentment, for the Wife has aimed her shafts at him directly, not in malice, but in mischievous defiance. Not only has she entered the lists as a disputant in theology, but she has gone out of her way to attack his order, railing at them especially for their satire on women. "No clerk," she declares, "can speak well of wives. It is an impossibility." And, worse than all, she has told how she had married a clerk of Oxford, an alumnus of our modest scholar's own university, and had reduced him to shameful subjection. The Wife is an heresiarch after her own boisterous fashion. She is not to be taken too seriously, but she deserves a rebuke; and who is so fit

[1] D. 469-473.

to administer it as the Clerk himself, whose orthodoxy is unflinching, and whose every word is "sownynge in moral vertu"? It is not our Clerk's way, however, to thrust himself forward. His turn will come, and meanwhile he rides quietly along, listening without comment, and biding his time.

It is for the more talkative Pilgrims to speak first. The Pardoner has already intervened, and now the Friar, when the Wife declares that her prologue is finished, and her story about to begin, shows his interest by a laughing comment: "Well, dame, this is a long preamble of a tale!" The Sumner rebukes him angrily: —

> "Lo," quod the Somonour, "Goddes armes two!
> A frere wol entremette hym everemo.
> Lo, goode men, a flye and eek a frere
> Wol falle in every dyssh and eek mateere.
> What spekestow of preambulacioun?
> What! amble, or trotte, or pees, or go sit doun!
> Thou lettest oure disport in this manere."

A bitter quarrel is well underway, when the Host checks it sternly and bids the Wife go on. "Willingly," she answers, "if this worthy friar will allow me." "By all means," says the Friar politely, and the tale proceeds.

There is no dispute between the Wife of Bath and the Friar. They understand each other perfectly. It was with women like her, wealthy and

respectable citizenesses, that the Friar, as the
Prologue tells us, liked to cultivate an acquaintance. He much prefers their society to that of
lazars and poor wretches in the suburbs. Their
interchange of courtesies, then, is amicable
enough, and the intrusion of the Sumner, in apparent defence of the Wife, is quite uncalled-for.
His object, of course, is to snub the Friar, between whom and himself there is intense professional jealousy. The Wife, for her part, has
no liking for sumners, who were quite as pervasive and unpopular in the middle ages as catch-
polls were in the eighteenth century, and she
ignores his unwelcome advocacy. Details like
this needed no footnotes for Chaucer's contemporary readers. They are, indeed, to be taken for
granted as part of the setting or background.

The Wife's tale of What Women most Desire is a famous old story, which is extant in
several versions. As she tells it, it becomes an
illustrative exemplum, to enforce the moral of
her sermon. Sovereignty over men is a woman's
ambition, and the knight of the Round Table,
who found himself in a strange dilemma, submitted his judgment to his wife's choice, with
the happiest result. He lived with her in perfect
joy till their life's end, — and so "I pray," concludes the Wife of Bath, "that those may die
early who will not yield themselves entirely to

petticoat government." Mediæval feminism has had its say. The sermon is finished, and the moral is driven home.

Thus far the Wife of Bath has had plain sailing. She has proved her case to her own satisfaction, by experience, by authority, and by an illustrative story; and nobody seems inclined to take her to task.

The Friar compliments her in a non-committal fashion, but turns off, with a clever transition, to assail the Sumner, at whom he had been looking "with a louring chere" even since that worthy had reproved him for laughing at the Wife's preamble. What follows, then, is a comic interlude, like that between Miller and Reeve at an earlier stage of the pilgrimage. The Friar tells a tale of a sumner who was carried off by the devil, and the Sumner, so angry that he stood up in his stirrups, retorts with an incomparable satire on begging friars, worked up on the basis of a trivial and sordid fabliau. Nowhere in the pilgrimage is the dramatic interplay of character more remarkable. For the Wife is the moving cause of the quarrel, though quite involuntarily. Harry Bailly, we note, has been content to drop the reins. The drama guides itself, moving on by virtue of the relations of the *dramatis personae*, their characters, and the logic of the situation. To all appearances the discussion of marriage has ended with the speaker who began it. The day's journey closes with the Sumner's Tale. The Host, at all events, has no thought of reopening the debate on matrimony when he calls upon the Clerk of Oxford to begin the entertainment next morning.

The Clerk has made no sign. He is as demure, the Host remarks, as a bride at her wedding breakfast. "Cheer up!" cries Harry, "this is no time to study. Tell us some merry tale, not in the high style, of which you are doubtless a master, but in plain language, so that we may all understand it."

"Sire Clerk of Oxenford," oure Hooste sayde,
"Ye ryde as coy and stille as dooth a mayde
Were newe spoused, sittynge at the bord;
This day ne herde I of youre tonge a word.
I trowe ye studie aboute som sophyme;
But Salomon seith 'every thyng hath tyme.'
For Goddes sake, as beth of bettre cheere!
It is no tyme for to studien heere.
Telle us som myrie tale, by youre fey!
For what man that is entred in a pley,
He nedes moot unto the pley assente.
But precheth nat, as freres doon in Lente,
To make us for oure olde synnes wepe,
Ne that thy tale make us nat to slepe.
Telle us som murie thyng of aventures.
Youre termes, youre colours, and youre figures,
Keepe hem in stoor til so be that ye endite
Heigh style, as whan that men to kynges write.
Speketh so pleyn at this tyme, we yow preye,
That we may understonde what ye seye."

The Oxford scholar yields a courteous assent, and begins the tale of Griselda, taught him at Padua by a noble clerk of Italy, one Francis Petrarch, who is now dead and buried. God rest his soul!

The story starts quite innocently. Not until it is well underway do the Pilgrims perceive the Clerk's drift. He is telling the tale of a patient and obedient wife, whose steadfast devotion to her husband was proof against every trial. With consummate art he is answering the Wife of Bath without appearing to take any notice either of her arguments or of her boisterous assault upon his order. "Clerks," she has declared, "cannot possibly speak well of wives." Yet here is one clerk, repeating the tale told him by another, and its theme is wifely fidelity and woman's fortitude under affliction.

We should not forget that the Clerk's Tale, like the Wife's long sermon, is addressed to the Canterbury Pilgrims, not to us, though we are privileged to overhear. We must not only listen, but look. In our mind's eye, we must see the Pilgrims, and watch their demeanor. Naturally, they are interested, and, equally of course, they understand what the Clerk is doing. He is replying to the Wife of Bath, — confuting her heresies, and at the same time vindicating his own order from her abusive raillery.

One can hardly conceive a more skilful method of replying. Its indirectness and deliberation are alike masterly. The Clerk is not talking about the Wife of Bath. His tale contains no personal allusions. It is, on the face of it, simply an affecting narrative which he chanced to hear from a learned friend in Italy, and which he supposes may interest his fellow-travellers. But, as the picture of Griselda grows slowly on the canvas, no Pilgrim can fail to recognize the complete antithesis to the Wife of Bath. Besides, however you and I may feel about it, to Chaucer's contemporaries the story was infinitely pathetic. One of Petrarch's friends broke down while reading it aloud, and could not continue, so deep was his emotion, but had to hand the manuscript to one of his retinue to finish. Another read it through unmoved, but only because he did not believe that there ever lived a wife so loving, so submissive, and so patient under affliction.

This point, in truth, — the incredibility of the example, — might have weakened its force as an answer to the Wife of Bath, if she were logically in a position to take advantage of such an objection. But this she cannot well do without abandoning her main thesis, that women are vastly superior to men. She might, to be sure, retort that the story proves too much, that it shows that men are unfit to have dominion over

their wives, since they abuse it so abominably.
But, before she can frame any retort whatever, — if, indeed, she is not too much affected
by the pathos to be mistress of her argumentative faculties, — the Clerk, who is a professional
logician and a conscientious moralist, makes all
debate impossible by explaining, in Petrarch's
words, the true lesson. " This story is not meant
as an exhortation to wives to be as patient as
Griselda, for that would transcend the powers
of human nature. It teaches all of us, men and
women alike, how we should submit ourselves
to the afflictions that God sends. The Marquis
Walter was a ruthless experimenter with souls.
God is not like that. The trials He sends are for
our good, and we should accept them with
Christian resignation."

> This storie is seyd, nat for that wyves sholde
> Folwen Grisilde as in humylitee,
> For it were inportable, though they wolde;
> But for that every wight, in his degree,
> Sholde be constant in adversitee
> As was Grisilde; therfore Petrak writeth
> This storie, which with heigh stile he enditeth.
>
> For, sith a womman was so pacient
> Unto a mortal man, wel moore us oghte
> Receyven al in gree that God us sent;
> For greet skile is, he preeve that he wroghte.
> But he ne tempteth no man that he boghte,
> As seith Seint Jame, if ye his pistel rede;
> He preeveth folk al day, it is no drede,

And suffreth us, as for oure excercise,
With sharpe scourges of adversitee
Ful ofte to be bete in sondry wise;
Nat for to knowe oure wyl, for certes he,
Er we were born, knew al oure freletee;
And for oure beste is al his governaunce.
Lat us thanne lyve in vertuous suffraunce.

Here is a remarkable situation. The Clerk has vindicated his order by praising women, and he has set up again the orthodox tenet of wifely obedience. But he has not said a word to the Wife of Bath, and, in the moral, he has expressly removed the story from the domain of controversy by asserting, in the plainest terms, that it is not a lesson for wives, but for Christians in general. If he drops the subject now, he has left the Wife of Bath unanswered after all.

But he does not drop the subject. He has a surprise in store for the would-be feminist heresiarch and for the whole company. Suddenly, without a moment's warning, he turns to the Wife of Bath, and, with an air of serene and smiling urbanity, offers to recite a song that he has just composed in her honor, and in honor of the sect which she represents and of which she has proved herself so doughty a champion:—"May God establish both her way of life and her principles; for the world would suffer if they should not prevail":—

"Whos lyf and al hire secte God mayntene
In heigh maistrie, and elles were it scathe."

And so he declaims his Envoy in praise of feminism. It is an address to all wise and prudent married women, exhorting them to follow the precepts and the practice of the Wife of Bath.

But o word, lordynges, herkneth er I go:
It were ful hard to fynde now-a-dayes
In al a toun Grisildis thre or two;
For if that they were put to swiche assayes,
The gold of hem hath now so badde alayes
With bras, that thogh the coyne be fair at ye,
It wolde rather breste a-two than plye.

For which heere, for the Wyves love of Bathe —
Whos lyf and al hire secte God mayntene
In heigh maistrie, and elles were it scathe —
I wol with lusty herte, fressh and grene,
Seyn yow a song to glade yow, I wene;
And lat us stynte of ernestful matere.
Herkneth my song that seith in this manere:

Grisilde is deed, and eek hire pacience,
And bothe atones buryed in Ytaille;
For which I crie in open audience,
No wedded man so hardy be t'assaille
His wyves pacience in trust to fynde
Grisildis, for in certein he shal faille.

O noble wyves, ful of heigh prudence,
Lat noon humylitee youre tonge naille,
Ne lat no clerk have cause or diligence
To write of yow a storie of swich mervaille
As of Grisildis pacient and kynde,
Lest Chichevache yow swelwe in hire entraille!

Folweth Ekko, that holdeth no silence,
But evere answereth at the countretaille.
Beth nat bidaffed for youre innocence,
But sharply taak on yow the governaille.
Emprenteth wel this lessoun in youre mynde,
For commune profit sith it may availle.

Ye archewyves, stondeth at defense,
Syn ye be strong as is a greet camaille;
Ne suffreth nat that men yow doon offense.
And sklendre wyves, fieble as in bataille,
Beth egre as is a tygre yond in Ynde;
Ay clappeth as a mille, I yow consaille.

Ne dreed hem nat, doth hem no reverence,
For though thyn housbonde armed be in maille,
The arwes of thy crabbed eloquence
Shal perce his brest, and eek his aventaille.
In jalousie I rede eek thou hym bynde,
And thou shalt make hym couche as doth a quaille.

If thou be fair, ther folk been in presence
Shewe thou thy visage and thyn apparaille;
If thou be foul, be fre of thy dispence;
To gete thee freendes ay do thy travaille;
Be ay of chiere as light as leef on lynde,
And lat hym care, and wepe, and wrynge, and waille!

The moment is completely dramatic. It is not
Chaucer who speaks, but the Clerk of Oxenford,
and every word is in perfect character. His
mock encomium is not only a masterpiece of
sustained and mordant irony; it is a marvellous
specimen of technical skill in metre, in diction,
and in vigorous and concentrated satire. None

but the Clerk, a trained rhetorician, could have composed it. None but the Clerk, a master of logic and a practised disputant, could have turned upon an opponent so adroitly. The home thrust comes when the guard is down. The Clerk is a moral philosopher, and he has proved both his earnestness and his competence. It is one of the humors of literature that this Envoy is traditionally judged a violation of dramatic propriety, as being out of accord with the Clerk's character. On the contrary, as we have seen, it is adjusted, with the nicest art, not only to his character, but also to the situation and the relations among the *dramatis personae*.

Heedless criticism has thrown the Wife's Prologue into the huge heap of satires on woman piled up by successive generations of mediæval poets. This indiscriminate procedure ignores the essential element that distinguishes the Canterbury Tales from the ordinary narrative and didactic poetry of the middle ages. The Wife of Bath is an individual expressing herself in character, not a stalking horse for a satirist's poisoned arrows. Her revelations apply to herself. To extend them to wives or women in general, is as ludicrous as it would be to interpret Iago's cynical speeches as Shakspere's satire on men and husbands. We may even take the Miller to witness: —

Ther been ful goode wyves many oon,
And evere a thousand goode ayeyns oon badde.
That knowestow wel thyself, but if thou madde.[1]

Similarly, the ironical Envoy is not to be taken as Chaucer's revolt against the false morality of Griselda's parable, but as the utterance of the Clerk, under quite particular circumstances. Nor is it, even on the Clerk's part, an attack on wives or women. It is simply a satirical encomium on a particular person, the obstreperous widow of Bath, and on any others who may choose to adopt her principles or join her heretical sect.

The dramatic connection between the Clerk's Envoy and the Merchant's Tale is especially close. The last line of the Clerk's ironical advice to wives — to let their husbands " care and weep and wring and wail" — is picked up by the Merchant in a despairing echo: —

"Wepyng and waylyng, care and oother sorwe
I knowe ynogh, on even and a-morwe,"
Quod the Marchant, "and so doon other mo
That wedded been."

" There is no likeness between my wife and Griselda! I have been married only two months, and I have suffered more than any bachelor in a lifetime!"

The tale that follows is one of the most remarkable in the whole collection, — not for the

---

[1] A. 3154-3156.

plot, which is an old indecorous jest, but for the savage and cynical satire with which the Merchant has loaded the story. We need not respect him, for he no longer respects himself; but we cannot be angry. He is a stately and dignified personage, the last man from whom so furious an outburst would be expected; but his disillusion has been sudden and complete. Habitually cautious, both in word and act, he has played the fool by marrying the wrong woman, and, now that excitement loosens his tongue, he goes all lengths, for he is half-mad with rage and shame.

Let us not mistake the purpose of the Merchant's satire. May, the young wife, is not so much its object as the dotard January, who has not a single redeeming feature. Man's folly is the Merchant's text, rather than woman's frailty; and all the time he is really castigating himself. Yet the tale is also, in substance, another reply to the Wife of Bath and her heresies. It is as if one of her many husbands had come back to earth to confute her by giving his own side of the case. Above all things, we must avoid the error of those critics who treat the Merchant as if he were Chaucer. Here, if ever, it is vitally necessary to bear the drama in mind.

The Host is somewhat startled at the Merchant's story. His own wife, he is glad to say, is true as any steel, shrew though she may be. But

he goes on jestingly to express, in strict confidence
— with all the Pilgrims listening — his wish that
he were out of wedlock bonds. He will not tell all
his wife's faults, for fear some woman in the company may blab when they all get back to Southwark. Besides, his wit would not suffice. The
list would "dizzy the arithmetic of memory."
Obviously, Harry Bailly, too, is having his little
fling at the Wife of Bath, who still holds the
centre of the stage as the only begetter of the
whole discussion.

> "Ey! Goddes mercy!" seyde oure Hooste tho,
> "Now swich a wyf I pray God kepe me fro!
> Lo, whiche sleightes and subtilitees
> In wommen been! for ay as bisy as bees
> Been they, us sely men for to deceyve,
> And from the soothe evere wol they weyve;
> By this Marchauntes tale it preveth weel.
> But doutelees, as trewe as any steel
> I have a wyf, though that she povre be,
> But of hir tonge a labbyng shrewe is she,
> And yet she hath an heep of vices mo;
> Therof no fors! lat alle swiche thynges go.
> But wyte ye what? In conseil be it seyd,
> Me reweth soore I am unto hire teyd.
> For, and I sholde rekenen every vice
> Which that she hath, ywis I were to nyce;
> And cause why, it sholde reported be
> And toold to hire of somme of this meynee, —
> Of whom, it nedeth nat for to declare,
> Syn wommen konnen outen swich chaffare;
> And eek my wit suffiseth nat therto,
> To tellen al, wherfore my tale is do."

Now, at length, the Host feels sure that the debate on matrimony has run its course. The topic of Marriage has been long enough before the Pilgrims. A tale of love, he thinks, would be a welcome relief, and for such a tale he calls upon the Squire, who, as he suggests, must be well acquainted with the subject: —

> "Squier, com neer, if it youre wille be,
> And sey somwhat of love; for certes ye
> Konnen theron as muche as any man."[1]

The Squire's Tale is the justly celebrated though fragmentary romance of Cambuscan and the Brazen Horse, to finish which Milton longed to call up Chaucer from the grave. It rouses the admiration of the Franklin, not more for its substance than for the eloquent style and courtly bearing of the narrator. The Franklin is a wealthy man, ambitious to found a family. He has a son whose low tastes are a grief to him, and he compliments the Squire on his "gentil-lesse," contrasting him rather piteously with the ungracious heir, who will be rich some day, but has no wish to grow up a gentleman. The Host is impatient, or pretends to be. Perhaps he is only trying to irritate the Franklin to recalcitrancy, with a view to the huge forfeit agreed upon beforehand, the sum total of the company's expenditure on the road. "A straw for your

---

[1] F. 1-3.

'gentillesse'!" he exclaims. "Come on, and tell
us a story!"

"Straw for youre gentillesse!" quod oure Hoost.
"What, Frankeleyn! pardee, sire, wel thou woost
That ech of yow moot tellen atte leste
A tale or two, or breken his biheste."
"That knowe I wel, sire," quod the Frankeleyn.
"I prey yow, haveth me nat in desdeyn,
Though to this man I speke a word or two."
"Telle on thy tale withouten wordes mo."
"Gladly, sire Hoost," quod he, "I wole obeye
Unto your wyl; now herkneth what I seye.
I wol yow nat contrarien in no wyse
As fer as that my wittes wol suffyse.
I prey to God that it may plesen yow;
Thanne woot I wel that it is good ynow."

The Franklin is not to be caught in any such
trap. He assents cordially, without a hint of
rebellion, and begins the tale of Arveragus and
Dorigen.

The Franklin, like the Clerk before him, has a
surprise ready for Harry Bailly and the Pilgrims.
He resumes the debate on Matrimony, which had
lapsed, to all appearances, with the Host's calling
upon the Squire for a tale of love; and he not
only resumes it, but carries it to a triumphant
conclusion by solving the problem. He solves it,
too, by an appeal to precisely that quality which
he so much admires in the Squire, and which the
Host has scoffed at him for mentioning — the
quality of "gentillesse."

This procedure on the Franklin's part is manifestly deliberate; it is not accident, but belongs to Chaucer's plan.

The Franklin, as we have noted, feels a wistful interest in "gentillesse" — a delightful old term which includes culture, good breeding, and generous sentiments, or, to borrow Osric's words to Hamlet, "the continent of what part a gentleman would see." Naturally, therefore, he selects a story that illustrates this quality. It involves a graceful compliment to two of the Pilgrims who have held the stage in this act of Chaucer's Human Comedy, for the plot turns on the competing generosity of a husband (who is a knight), a lover (who is a squire), and a magician (who is a clerk), the appraisal of merit being left to the audience.

In itself, this tale, which is an old one, throws no light on the problem of sovereignty in marriage. At the outset, however, the Franklin makes a definite application. Arveragus, a noble knight of Brittany, wins the love of the lady Dorigen, who "takes him for her husband and her lord." Out of pure gentillesse, he promises that he will never assert his authority after they are married, but will continue to be her humble servant, as a lover ought to be to his lady. In return for this gentillesse, Dorigen vows never to abuse her sway, but to be his true and obedient wife.

Thus the married lovers dwell together in perfect accord, each deferring to the other, and neither claiming the sovereignty; and it is this relation of mutual love and forbearance, the outcome of gentillesse, that carries them safely through the entanglements of the plot and preserves their wedded happiness unimpaired as long as they live.

Love and marriage, according to the courtly system, were held to be incompatible, since marriage involves mastery on the husband's part, and mastery drives out love.

> Non bene conveniunt, nec in una sede morantur,
> Maiestas et amor.

This theory the Franklin utterly repudiates. In true marriage, he argues, there should be no assertion of sovereignty on either side. Love must be the controlling principle, — perfect, gentle love, which brings forbearance with it. Such is his solution of the whole problem, and thus he concludes the long debate begun by that jovial heresiarch, the Wife of Bath.

> Thus been they bothe in quiete and in reste.
> For o thyng, sires, saufly dar I seye,
> That freendes everych oother moot obeye,
> If they wol longe holden compaignye.
> Love wol nat been constreyned by maistrye.
> Whan maistrie comth, the God of Love anon
> Beteth his wynges, and farewel, he is gon!

Love is a thyng as any spirit free.
Wommen, of kynde, desiren libertee,
And nat to been constreyned as a thral;
And so doon men, if I sooth seyen shal.
Looke who that is moost pacient in love,
He is at his avantage al above.
Pacience is an heigh vertu, certeyn,
For it venquysseth, as thise clerkes seyn,
Thynges that rigour sholde nevere atteyne.
For every word men may nat chide or pleyne.
Lerneth to suffre, or elles, so moot I goon,
Ye shul it lerne, wher so ye wole or noon;
For in this world, certein, ther no wight is
That he ne dooth or seith somtyme amys.
Ire, siknesse, or constellacioun,
Wyn, wo, or chaungynge of complexioun
Causeth ful ofte to doon amys or speken.
On every wrong a man may nat be wreken.
After the tyme moste be temperaunce
To every wight that kan on governaunce.
And therfore hath this wise, worthy knyght,
To lyve in ese, suffrance hire bihight,
And she to hym ful wisly gan to swere
That nevere sholde ther be defaute in here.
  Heere may men seen an humble, wys accord;
Thus hath she take hir servant and hir lord,
Servant in love and lord in mariage.
Thanne was he bothe in lordshipe and servage.
Servage? nay, but in lordshipe above,
Sith he hath bothe his lady and his love;
His lady, certes, and his wyf also,
The which that lawe of love acordeth to.
And whan he was in this prosperitee,
Hoom with his wyf he gooth to his contree,
Nat fer fro Pedmark, ther his dwellyng was,
Where as he lyveth in blisse and in solas.
  Who koude telle, but he hadde wedded be,

The joye, the ese, and the prosperitee
That is bitwixe an housbonde and his wyf?[1]

There is no mistaking Chaucer's purpose in
this, the final scene of that act of the Canterbury
Pilgrimage which deals with the problem of husband and wife. He does not allow the Franklin
to tell a tale without a moral expressed and to
leave the application to our powers of inference.
On the contrary, the Franklin's discussion of the
subject is both definite and compendious. It
extends to nearly a hundred lines, without a
particle of verbiage, and occupies a conspicuous
position at the very beginning of the story, so
that the tale is utilized to illustrate and enforce
the principle. And in the course of this discussion the Franklin alludes, in a way that cannot
have escaped his fellow-travellers, to the Wife of
Bath's harangue on the thraldom of husbands,[2]
to the patience of Griselda [3] and the theories of
the Marquis Walter as described by the Clerk
of Oxford,[4] and to the grimly ironical praise of
wedlock which makes lurid the frenzied satire
of the disillusioned Merchant.[5] It is clear, therefore, that Chaucer means us to regard the Franklin as "knitting up the matter," as summarizing
the whole debate and bringing it to a definitive

---

[1] F. 760–805.   [2] F. 769–770.
[3] F. 771.   [4] F. 768–769.
[5] F 803–805; cf. E. 1337-1341.

conclusion which we are to accept as a perfect rule of faith and practice.

In assigning to the Franklin this supremely important office, Chaucer acted with his usual perspicacity. Marriage, when all is said and done, is an affair of practical life. Theorists may talk about it, — divines, philosophers, men of law, harpers harping with their harps, — but we listen with a certain skepticism when they take high ground, or shut their eyes to the weakness of human nature. To the Franklin, on the contrary, we lend a credent ear. He is no cloistered rhetorician, but a ruddy, white-bearded vavasour, a great man in his neighborhood, fond of the good things of life and famous for his lavish hospitality. He has been sheriff of his county and Member of Parliament, and is perpetual presiding justice at the sessions of the peace. Such a man lies under no suspicion of transcendental theorism or vague heroics. When *he* speaks of mutual forbearance and perfect gentle love between husband and wife, we listen with conviction. The thing is possible. The problem need puzzle us no longer.

> Who koude telle, but he hadde wedded be,
> The joye, the ese, and the prosperitee
> That is bitwixe an housbonde and his wyf?

Chaucer has fared hard at the hands of some of his biographers. They are determined to take his jesting seriously, and his serious words in jest. Let us try to be candid. We know that Chaucer was married, but we know nothing whatever of the happiness or unhappiness of his married life. Not a single external fact has come down to us that throws any light on this question. We may believe as we list, but we should, in all conscience, not pick up a word here and a phrase there — now a joke about St. Leonard, copied from the Romance of the Rose, and now a comic address to Bukton, suited to the rough jocosity of a farewell bachelor dinner — we should not, I say, piece together these shreds and patches of humor and call our motley fabric autobiography, while all the time we disregard the significance of a whole act of Chaucer's Human Comedy of the Canterbury Pilgrimage containing more than six thousand verses of his very best work!

The most abandoned character among the Canterbury Pilgrims is the Pardoner, and the cynicism with which he boasts of his infamy has often been cited as an example of Chaucer's heedless or defiant violation of dramatic propriety. Some have tried to justify the poet on the plea of *in vino veritas*. But the Pardoner is quite sober. No draught of "moist and corny ale" will account for his self-revelation. He knows precisely what he is about when he exposes the horrid hypocrisy of his professional life. Why does he do it?

The Doctor has just told the tragic story of Virginia, by which the Host is profoundly affected. He feels the need of a merry tale, and so he calls upon the Pardoner: —

> Thou beel amy, thou Pardoner," he sayde,
> "Telle us som myrthe or japes right anon."
>   "It shal be doon," quod he, "by Seint Ronyon!
> But first," quod he, "heere at this ale-stake
> I wol bothe drynke, and eten of a cake."

What the host wants is a ribald story, and the Pardoner is quite ready to accommodate him. But the gentlefolk object, and call for a tale of morality: —

> "Nay, lat hym telle us of no ribaudye!
> Telle us som moral thyng, that we may leere
> Som wit, and thanne wol we gladly heere."

For this the Pardoner is equally ready, — but he is not to be cheated out of his refreshment: —

> "I graunte, ywis," quod he, "but I moot thynke
> Upon som honest thyng while that I drynke."

Absurdity sometimes goes far in literary criticism, but I think it has "made its masterpiece" — in a small way, as one carves a grotesque out of a peach stone — in the notion that the Pardoner is obliged to stop and think before he can recollect an edifying story. Why! he is a "noble ecclesiast"; his livelihood depends on his abilities as a popular preacher, and no sermon was complete without an illustrative anecdote. True, the Pardoner himself pretends to require a moment's reflection in order to turn his mind away from merriment to serious subjects. But he merely continues the course of thought which began at the moment when the Host called on him for a tale (a merry one, be it remembered), and the subject of his meditations is simply *cakes and ale*, which he is determined to have before telling any story whatsoever.

The company, we should remember, is just passing one of the many roadside booths where ale and wheaten wafers were dispensed to travellers, and we are not to imagine that the Pardoner is the only member of the band who stands in need of a little sustenance. Indeed, the first suggestion comes from Harry himself, who thinks that a tankard may relieve the spasm of heartache that the Physician's tragic story has brought on.

Now this lively dialogue gives us the key to the situation quite as satisfactorily, I should think, as if it were one of Mr. Bernard Shaw's interminable stage-directions. The Pilgrims are well acquainted with the Pardoner by this time, for he is on a vacation, and has made no attempt to hide his colors. This acquaintance is shown clearly by the Host's request for a "merry tale,"

by the Pardoner's hearty assent, and by the
instant protest of the "gentles." The sudden
change from the proposed ribald story to one of
high morality is, then, the dramatic occasion of
the Pardoner's long preamble, which contains
the cynical avowal that so worries the critics.
True, this prologue is cast into a conventional
form, — that of the Confession, in which some
typical figure is regularly made to satirize his
type by speaking in the first person. But here,
as ever in Chaucer, the convention is vitalized,
and it is an individual that speaks, not a type.
Our Pardoner is a famous pulpit orator, and he
is about to repeat one of his best sermons. He
knows that he shall preach with fervor, because
he has the histrionic temperament, and also
because the tale is so moving that no one could
tell it flippantly. Besides, he is proud of his eloquence, and has no mind to spoil his discourse
by slipshod delivery.

Under these circumstances, the cynical frankness of the Pardoner is dramatically inevitable.
He is simply forestalling the reflections of his
fellow-pilgrims. "I know I am a rascal," he says
in effect, "and *you* know it; and I wish to show
you that I know you know it!" Like many another of us poor mortals, the Pardoner is willing
to pass for a knave, but objects to being taken
for a fool. To deceive mankind is his business,

but this time no deception is possible, and he scorns the rôle of a futile hypocrite.

The exemplum which the sermon embodies is one of the best in the world, and comes from the Orient, where it is still in popular circulation. It tells the fate of the three revellers who sally forth to kill Death. I have already mentioned it, in my first lecture, where I spoke of the skill that Chaucer shows in the resolution after the climax. Further detail is unnecessary, for the tale is very familiar to modern readers. Still, I must dwell for a moment on one passage, which affords a remarkable illustration of effective reticence.

The aged wayfarer whom the three rioters encounter, and whom they treat with such rudeness, is undoubtedly Death in person. But Chaucer does not say so. He describes him as an old, old man who cannot die. This old man directs the rioters to the tree under which lies the fatal treasure, and passes on his way, with the grimly significant remark, "I moot go thider as I have to go." Death, of course, has his own affairs to attend to during this pestilence season, and the rioters are his, safe enough: they have but to follow his directions, and covetousness will provide for that! And so the tragedy proceeds without delay to its inexorable conclusion.

The Pardoner knows his sermon by heart (he

has told us as much), and its momentum carries him beyond the point at which, on this particular occasion, he ought to have stopped, — carries him, indeed, so far that he appends his customary summons to come up to the chancel, make offering to the relics, and receive absolution. This summons is quite in order when he is preaching to the villagers in some country church, but now he realizes, when once it is uttered, that it is inopportune enough in the present company, who have no illusions about either his relics or himself. And so he cynically reminds his fellow-travellers of what he told them at the outset, — that he is merely giving them a specimen of his pulpit oratory: "And lo, sires, thus I preche!"

Then, suddenly, unexpectedly, without an instant's warning, his cynicism falls away, and he utters the solemn words: "May Christ, the physician of our souls, grant you His pardon, for that is better than mine! I will not deceive you, though I get my living by fraud!"

> I yow assoille, by myn heigh power,
> Yow that wol offre, as clene and eek as cleer
> As ye were born. — And lo, sires, thus I preche.
> And Jhesu Crist, that is oure soules leche,
> So graunte yow his pardoun to receyve,
> For that is best; I wol yow nat deceyve.

The Pardoner has not always been an assassin of souls. He is a renegade, perhaps, from some holy order. Once he preached for Christ's sake; and now, under the spell of the wonderful story he has told and of recollections that stir within him, he suffers a very paroxysm of agonized sincerity. It can last but a moment. The crisis passes, and the reaction follows. He takes refuge from himself in a wild orgy of reckless jesting: — "But see here, my friends! I forgot to tell you about my relics. Here they are — the best in England — and first-rate pardons, too! It's a regular insurance policy to have a Pardoner like me in the company. Come up, and make your offerings. You first, Sir Host! for I'm sure you are the worst sinner in the troop."

Harry Bailly has no conception (how could he?) of the Pardoner's emotional crisis. He answers with rough jocularity; but he means no offence, and, under ordinary circumstances the Pardoner would simply have paid him tit for tat. But the moment is too intense for poise. With another revulsion of feeling, the Pardoner becomes furiously angry, so angry that words stick in his throat.

> This Pardoner answerde nat a word;
> So wrooth he was, no word ne wolde he seye.
> "Now," quod oure Hoost, "I wol no lenger pleye
> With thee, ne with noon oother angry man."

"I won't joke," cries the Host indignantly, "with a man that cannot keep his temper."

Then the Knight interposes to make up the quarrel. They are reconciled amidst the laughter of the company. For nobody but Geoffrey Chaucer divined the tragic face behind the satyr's mask, — Geoffrey Chaucer, poet, idealist, burgher of London, Commissioner of Dykes and Ditches, who loved his fellow-men, both good and bad, and found no answer to the puzzle of life but in truth and courage and beauty and belief in God.

THE END

INDEX

INDEX